BOOK 3:
TEAM PERFORMANCE

HELLEN WARD

About City & Guilds

City & Guilds is the UK's leading provider of vocational qualifications, offering over 500 awards across a wide range of industries, and progressing from entry level to the highest levels of professional achievement. With over 8500 centres in 100 countries, City & Guilds is recognised by employers worldwide for providing qualifications that offer proof of the skills they need to get the job done.

Equal opportunities

City & Guilds fully supports the principle of equal opportunities and we are committed to satisfying this principle in all our activities and published material. A copy of our equal opportunities policy statement is available on the City & Guilds website.

Copyright

First edition 2012

ISBN 978 0 85193 215 6

Publisher Louise Le Bas
Cover design by Gloo Communications
Typeset by Select Typesetters Ltd
Printed in the UK by CLOC

Publications

For information about or to order City & Guilds support materials, contact 0844 534 0000 or centresupport@cityandguilds.com. You can find more information about the materials we have available at www.cityandguilds.com/publications.

Every effort has been made to ensure that the information contained in this publication is true and correct at the time of going to press. However, City & Guilds' products and services are subject to continuous development and improvement and the right is reserved to change products and services from time to time. City & Guilds cannot accept liability for loss or damage arising from the use of information in this publication.

City & Guilds
1 Giltspur Street
London EC1A 9DD

T 0844 543 0033
www.cityandguilds.com
publishingfeedback@cityandguilds.com

CONTENTS

ACKNOWLEDGEMENTS

I would like to thank L'Oréal Professionnel for their help and support throughout my hairdressing career, particularly Neil Cornay, Commercial Director, who is now both a friend and a great ally in our on-going relationship with a great supplier; Gill Pope, Educational Development Director, whose belief in the educational value of my business knowledge is unwavering; and Sam at Essence PR for our on-going partnership spanning over a decade.

I could not have written this book without the guidance and advice of Dean Laming, from Salon Gold Insurance, Paul Mattei and Terry Marchant at The Leaman Partnership, our accountants, and Jeremy Wakeling, our surveyor whose relationship has been invaluable throughout our dealings with landlords. I would like to thank my business associate at Ultimate Salon Management.com – John Jameson, for being the geekiest, brainiest and loveliest teccy on the planet. There are many people I admire greatly in this industry, and none more than the Phillip Rogers, Chairman of HABB and a true philanthropist as well as being the business driving force behind the Sassoon empire for many years, and Simon Ostler, ex-MD of Tigi and now working on his own projects, whose drive, determination and business expertise are second to none in this industry.

My team are always my rocks – my PA Sam Good for her unbelievable brainpower, myriad of skills and unending patience; Gavin Hoare, our Salon Manager for being the best in the business and the face of the salon and above all, our General Manager Julie Norman, who alongside me, not only helped formulate all the elements of this book during our two decade working relationship, but puts them into practice daily and never fails to be a constancy in my life, both personally and professionally. Also thanks to our wonderful management team at the salon; Mario, Nando, Crissy, Matt, Gina, Lou and Candice who help me take all the credit for our wonderful business.

Above all, I want to thank Richard, the best husband and father on the planet – whose goals, dreams and vision I never stop sharing; my father Peter and my mother Lorna for teaching me everything I know before I realised I needed to know it, and all my family for their love and support, including my children Elysia and Oliver, who I hope will follow in our footsteps one day.

Hellen Ward

Picture credits

Every effort has been made to acknowledge all copyright holders as below and publishers will, if notified, correct any errors in future editions.

Courtesy of Ann Herman: p7; **Blushes:** p86; **Cambridge Regional College:** pp96, 189, 214; **HM Revenue & Customs:** pp49, 50; **iStockphoto.com:** © -Antonio- pp75, 80; © 3DStock p142; © 3dts p101; © alexskopje p177; © alexsl pp121, 132; © AnthiaCumming p172; © arcady_31 p172; © ArtisticCaptures p81; © cenix p129; © courtneyk p112; © DaddyBit p80; © DNY59 pp115, 123, 159; © DOConnell p96; © Elenathewise p148; © Elnur p188; © fabiopb p106; © fotofrog p185; © GordonBellPhotography p201; © iqoncept p162; © ISerg p99; © IvelinRadkov p131; © JamesBrey p199; © jandrielombard p206; © JazzIRT pp83, 214; © Jitalia17 p42; © JulNichols p64; © KLH49 p168; © MarcoMarchi p210; © marekuliasz p127; © MarkSwallow p149; © mattjeacock p31; © MCCAIG p53; © mediaphotos pp129, 131; © MJHollinshead p156; © Mordolff p125; © Nikada p219; © pagadesign pp58, 151, 210; © PashaIgnatov p20; © pearleye p134; © Pears2295 pp157, 164; © peepo p22; © PeskyMonkey p124; © PinkTag p161; © pixdeluxe p168; © PlushStudios p83; © powerofforever p89; © RapidEye p196; © RTimages p153; © RuslanDashinsky p133; © selimaksan p32; © ShevchenkoN p191; © shirhan p56; © surfertide p21; © tattywelshie p50; © terrymorris p102; © Thinglass p184; © Tommydickson p116; © traveler1116 p213; © travellinglight p134; © urbanglimpses p122; © vm p191; © Warchi p84; © wragg pp126, 217; © wwing p190; © youngvet p110; © Yuri_Arcurs p142; Jon Bradley p197; **L'ORÉAL:** 88; **Richard Ward Hair & Metrospa:** pp6, 18, 24, 27, 36, 44, 47, 55, 65, 62, 91, 91, 145, 170, 185, 211, 221; **The London School of Beauty Therapy:** p66, 86, 92, 93, 204; **TONI&GUY:** pp90, 146.

ABOUT THE AUTHOR

Hellen Ward is co-owner of the Richard Ward brand, together with her husband, Celebrity Hairdresser Richard. Hellen started her hairdressing career after leaving school at 16, doing an apprenticeship with a national chain. After working a column for a couple of years, Hellen was promoted to Salon Manager, then Regional Manager and finally General Manager of Harrods Hair and Beauty at the tender age of 23, before finally meeting Richard and opening their own business in 1992. Combining Hellen's business acumen with Richard's artistic skills, they have gone on to create one of the most successful, independently owned hair and beauty companies in the UK. Hellen lectures and educates hair and beauty salon owners, both nationally and internationally, as well as running other companies outside the hair and beauty field. She has two children and lives in London.

Hellen Ward

FOREWORD

As a seasoned ex-hairdresser and salon owner, now wearing my hat as Show Coordinator and Events Chairman for the Fellowship for British Hairdressing; if there's one thing I understand it's the importance of teamwork and getting your team to work to its best. And that is exactly what this book is all about.

Hellen addresses all aspects of creating, managing, growing and developing a team and looks at installing a structure, systems and procedures to monitor and improve everyone's individual performance.

So whether you're about to open your first salon or are an experienced manager, this book will give you a real understanding of what's needed to maximise salon performance. It will guide you to review and refresh your current working practices to ensure you stay ahead of the game in our ever competitive, evolving industry.

Hellen Ward is a lady I admire greatly for her business acumen and her commitment to the greater good of the salon industry. Her wise trouble-shooting, commercial and financial advice – all delivered in her trademark no nonsense, straight-talking style – means her business intelligence is much in demand; no wonder she is referred to as our 'business guru'.

So read, absorb and put into practice everything this book suggests. For your salon's success – I can't recommend it highly enough.

Ann Herman
(Fellowship of British Hairdressing).

INTRODUCTION

Never has there been a better time to be in the hair and beauty industry!

Industry statistics tell us that our sector is showing sustained growth and that there are more than 35,000 salons in the UK alone. These employ more than 245,000 hairdressers, barbers, hair technicians, beauty therapists and nail technicians in an industry that is worth over £5.25 billion per annum. The average price of services in our salons has increased by 90% over the last 10 years and, with the heightened media awareness about our profession, many hairdressers are becoming celebrities in their own right – with multi-million pound product ranges, brand endorsements and franchise businesses continuing to evolve and develop. Hairdressing has shaken off its image of being badly paid, lowly or servile and has reinvented itself as a credible, creative profession with a multitude of spin-off careers: PR, media, marketing, sales and commercial management, brand management, technical training, franchising and personal development, to name but a few.

This is all very impressive, but working in the hair and beauty industry is not easy. As has been found by the owners of the many small businesses (classified as employing 50 or fewer staff) that make up 80% of British workforce employers, the expertise needed to run your own company is ever-growing. Running a salon involves many different skills. We need to have an understanding of HR, PR, marketing, training and education, and retailing and merchandising, as well as an aptitude for the finances and commercial negotiations if we want our businesses to thrive.

The work is labour intensive, with the staff payroll being our biggest expense but also our greatest asset – and one that needs careful nurturing and cultivating. Failure to do this can result in heightened staff turnover; this is one of the biggest risks to the financial security of our businesses, and arguably the surest way to potentially lose turnover and profits. We are hugely dependent on our team staying with us and building successful client relationships through delivering personal, one-to-one service. Constant, ongoing training and staff development is therefore essential.

In order to ensure precious rebookings and word-of-mouth recommendations, technical standards need to be second to none, client service must be flawless and the customer experience unrivalled. The industry is uniquely client-facing, so customer satisfaction is key. Yet research tells us that client loyalty levels are dropping. UK salons have over 80 million visits per year but, with 98% of unhappy clients switching salons instead of complaining, we have our work cut out to ensure standards are up to scratch.

In an increasingly competitive marketplace, branding and PR must be well-researched and marketed if we are to succeed. The profession is constantly evolving, so being on top of trends is ever more vital; we need to research client demand for new technologies and innovations in the market if we want to keep our customers loyal. Merchandising and retailing can bring in large revenue streams which can be a vital part of our businesses. But positioning your brand against the competition is increasingly complex, as the market is in continued growth, with salons becoming more and more innovative and sophisticated and standards everywhere constantly improving.

Most salon managers or owners have worked their way up from apprentice level, honing their talents creatively and usually deciding to open their own salons because they are the busiest and best stylist or therapist. However, this may mean that sometimes the business side of things can get a little overlooked. All that wonderful, carefully cultivated creativity can mean we are less interested in the financial, commercial side of things. So it is no surprise then that statistics show some 1200 salons a year going out of business – with poor management skills being one of the most likely reasons. Managing a salon is a complex business and many would-be salon owners find there is a real lack of resources and practical help on hand.

From my own experience, most of what we learn is gleaned by living through the situations ourselves; this is certainly how it has been for me. I have had no formal management training or university education. I started as an apprentice and worked my way up to being a stylist, salon manager, then regional manager before finally opening my own business when I was in my mid-twenties. I had no official training, and there were no management books like this one that had been written by someone with a real understanding of what it is like to be a salon manager or owner. In fact, I often left meetings with my accountant feeling unsure of what he was telling me because I was too embarrassed to ask him questions or admit that I was baffled by his terminology! I am sure I am not alone in this and that many of you need to know some basic financial facts so you can understand your own finances – even if you are not directly handling them yourselves.

What my career has given me is a diverse experience of every type of salon imaginable. I have managed salons with 125 staff in some of the country's most glamorous department stores, as well as salons with just two staff in less salubrious locations. I have worked with salon managers up and down the country and experienced many different hairdressers, therapists and clienteles. I have worked hard to learn what made them all tick and understand the issues they faced. There were often many similarities, although sometimes the problems they encountered could not have been more different. *Everything* I have learned has come through experience; this is what I am sharing with you in the course of this series of books.

My *Ultimate Guide to Salon Management* is here to 'hold your hand' and guide you through the complexities of owning or running a salon or spa. I am not a lawyer, solicitor, accountant, wizard mathematician or business genius, and obviously there is *never* any substitute for proper legal advice, but I am a successful salon owner and entrepreneur. My 'tried-and-tested' formule and techniques can help to give you the systems and tools you need to ensure your business runs as smoothly as possible. I can tell you a little about everything you will need to know to run a salon well, but some subjects are so comprehensive that it is not possible to cover them in enough detail in a book like this. What I can give you is a snapshot overview and general understanding of all the areas you need to think about in order to really manage your business to the best of your ability.

It can be a lonely affair being a boss, but sometimes just knowing that we all experience the same dilemmas, issues and problems may be enough to give you the confidence to get where you want to go – or just point you in the right direction.

In my series of three books, we look at the following key areas:
- Getting Established
- Managing Finances
- Team Performance

In *Getting Established*, Part 1 covers the nuts and bolts of what you need to know to open a salon – the setting up and the red tape aspects. Even if you are already established, reading this guide will act as a reference and a checklist to make sure you have got it all covered. If you are a salon manager, you may not need to actually undertake the tasks involved with setting up but you will undoubtedly need to understand them as they will continue to be part of your job role. In Part 2, we look at finding your own brand identity and conveying that to your customers in the branding, marketing and PR sections. These vital elements of establishing your business image will become the blueprint for your planning and brand evolvement.

In the second book, *Managing Finances*, Part 1 looks at increasing turnover and my tried-and-tested check lists to make sure your productivity is maximised. In Part 2 we cover the equally vital area of controlling costs, to make sure your salon is as profitable as possible. Both elements are covered with hints and tips from my own business experience to ensure you are focused on the right areas to grow and develop your business.

In this third book, *Team Performance*, the first part is dedicated to creating and managing a team, using my systems to ensure that your team really is your biggest asset. Part 2 will look at monitoring team financial performance, ensuring your team are delivering to the best of their ability and you are tracking and evaluating their performance. The series is then complete and will hopefully provide you with a reference guide to every area you need to think about to manage your salon successfully.

Each book is full of tips, facts and examples to demonstrate the strategies that I have implemented in my 25 years of salon management. The aim is to demystify each element to make it easy to understand and introduce in your salons, and so enable you to maximise the productivity and profitability of your business. You will also find my '10 steps' – a set of golden rules and quick reference points to sum up the secrets of creating a brand, a profitable salon and steps to success. All of the books are written in 'hair and beauty speak', avoiding jargon and psycho-babble with my dos and don'ts, useful words, tips and facts to help make understanding salon management as easy as possible and give you the complete guide to making your salon the best it can be.

Good luck and here's to many more entrepreneurs in our sector!

(Statistics courtesy of HABIA and L'Oréal Professionnel)

TEAM PERFORMANCE

This handbook is the last of my series of three, and looks at human resources within a hair or beauty salon. It will help you to get the most out of your most vital asset – your teams – and to maximise staff retention and optimise individual performance to benefit your salon's profitability and productivity.

PREFACE

Our appetite for hair, beauty, nail and spa trend has never been so strong. We have never been more influenced, as consumers, by different style innovations and developments. From celebrity looks to media images and catwalk trends, these modes that affect us all are increasingly as much about hair and make-up as they are about fashion, and can impact our whole culture.

We tend to think of this as a new development but, actually, hair and beauty looks have always been at the forefront of what defines the times. In a similar way to fashion, the changes and innovations in make-up and hair styles have become some of the defining elements in our history. Whole dynasties and eras have been defined by different hair and beauty trends: from Cleopatra's blunt fringe, geometric cut and kohl-rimmed eyes to the severely whitened face of Queen Elizabeth 1st. Hair and beauty looks can help to define our eras and become iconic style statements of the times they represent.

Not only are they a sign of different fashions and trends, but hair and beauty styles can be symbolic of a more general historical significance. During the Second World War, British women were renowned for 'tanning' their legs with teabags, and drawing in stocking seams with eyebrow pencils when they could not get hold of new stockings. This industriousness and frugality underlined the austere times through which people were living, as echoed by the severe and neatly styled hair looks that were evident.

Lately, with the growing trend for celebrities and the insatiable desire to emulate their latest looks and fashions, the hair and beauty business has become an integral part of the British economy. In 1996, when Jennifer Anniston's 'Rachel' cut from the US TV series *Friends* became so popular, the upsurge in trade was significant and long lasting. Similarly, Victoria and David Beckham have led both female and male trends and, more importantly, created new markets in male grooming and self-tanning, as well as pioneering iconic looks such as the Pob. Like other style icons, such as supermodel Linda Evangelista and the singer Madonna, Victoria Beckham's fondness for constantly evolving and changing her image through hair innovations, such as extensions, have resulted in new multi-million pound industries that have helped to shape our sector's economy.

Key events in British history have also shared their limelight with hair and beauty trends – who can forget Princess Diana's fresh and dewy wedding make-up? Or consider the stunning bridal hair of the Duchess of Cambridge, the former Kate Middleton, which signified the creation of the demi-chignon and has become the style of choice for brides the world over. These significant historical events have helped to create the trends that have impacted our economy and influenced signature styles for years to come.

With the world becoming more accessible through easy and low-cost travel and tourism, there has been a growing trend for a whole new area of spa and hairdressing facilities – from airport lounges to cruise liners. Salons are a 'must-have' service, and the importance of keeping ourselves looking good wherever we are has not been lost to the hoteliers and hospitality industry. The concept of wanting accessible grooming is ever-growing. The younger generation's insatiable appetite for brow bars, threading bars, spray-tanning salons and conventional hair and beauty salons is ever-increasing. There is a new and more comprehensive attitude to grooming among this demographic, which is being catered for in ever more industrious ways. The desire for ever more sophisticated salons and facilities to cater for the growing male grooming market are evident and increasingly sophisticated.

Who knows what the next iconic trend will be that will influence our salons over the coming years? One thing is for sure, as salon managers and owners, our increasingly entrepreneurial thinking and professionalism will ensure we maximise the resulting commercial opportunities.

PART 1
INTRODUCTION:
CREATING
AND MANAGING
A TEAM

In Part 1 of this final book of my series, we will look at how to put together your dream team – from interviewing and recruiting staff, to devising salary packages and contracts of employment. We will focus on getting all the ingredients together to create your ultimate salon staff and, most importantly, how to keep them.

Our teams are the key to the success of our salons – salon customers are just as loyal to their hairdresser, technician or therapist as they are to our salon brand. Therefore, retaining team members must be the focus of any salon or spa manager or owner. In this book we will look at the systems and structure you can put in place to keep your staff turnover to a minimum.

In this part of the book, we will look at putting your team together. First, we will cover recruiting and selecting your team, then we will look at the obligations and requirements you need to implement and understand as an employer. Staff training and development are key to this, so we will cover the structure of your salon and roles and responsibilities in your team. Excellence in customer service is essential – so we will look at how you can develop your team to deliver the highest standards in client care, and what systems and brand ethos you can introduce to make your client experience the best it can be.

Unfortunately, you cannot guarantee that things will always go well, so we will also cover how to understand and implement disciplinary procedures in order to get the right result; educating and developing your team's performance. To do any of this, your leadership skills are vital, so we will look at how to develop your managerial style and ensure you are always the role model you should be to your team.

CHAPTER 1
INTERVIEWING AND RECRUITMENT

This chapter covers what you need to think about when recruiting your team, as well as the most effective methods for attracting potential staff. We will look at how to develop great interviewing techniques and communication styles and how to deal with recruitment. We will also consider how to put together an effective induction programme, to get new team members thinking the right way, and issuing them with job descriptions to ensure they know what you expect of them.

THE DREAM TEAM?

Finding your 'dream team' is not easy. Just as in our personal relationships, some staff will naturally gel with you and your salon ethos, and others simply will not connect – no matter how you try. Finding the right people to work with you is key. We spend most of our lives at work, and a happy salon is a productive one. I always say that, as the boss, I need to feel happy and relaxed among my team; if I do not, then something (or someone) is wrong. An unhappy staffroom means an unhappy client experience, so it is vital that we get the mix right. A good team will feel like a comfortable pair of slippers – you will understand their weaknesses and live with them (even if you try and influence them!) and you will celebrate, nurture and capitalise on their strengths.

For your ideal team, it is far easier if you can 'grow your own'. But cultivating and training a staff team to echo your ethos is a long-term plan, not a short-term fix. You will need to put in a lot of hard work to ensure you get the right results, and you will have to be incredibly patient; it will take years for your fledgling team to fully blossom when they are at senior level and for you to reap the rewards of building your foundations.

Even if you develop and train as many team members as possible, you will always need to recruit team members who you cannot train yourself, like therapists and receptionists. Where possible, however, try to encourage the 'breeding' and evolution of your senior staff by investing in them at a junior level, so that apprentice hairdressers and technicians are schooled into your way of doing things from day one. This means that the all-important settling in period is already covered, and they have only ever known your way of doing things. Other team members who have more experience of salons and the world of work will need more time to integrate and get out of bad habits, so learning what to look for and judging those who will naturally 'fit' at interview stage is vital.

RECRUITMENT

First, you must effectively judge that you have sufficient work or business to warrant the new recruit. It may be that you are replacing a member of staff who has left, or that business has grown sufficiently to employ an extra team member. Before you recruit, you need to be sure that the extra work could not be absorbed by another member of staff, or there are no internal recruits who could fill the position. I always let the existing team know of any vacancies within the salon, to enable them to apply personally if they wish. It might be, for example, that you are recruiting at management level and there are some candidates among your existing team who would apply if they had known of the vacancy or been given the chance. Doing this also takes away the element of people being 'anti' the new role, as you can always say that all applications were considered.

Make sure you can always say that all applications were considered fairly.

METHODS OF RECRUITMENT

There are several ways in which you can recruit new team members. Increasingly, the internet is probably the most effective and easiest way to advertise vacancies, but word of mouth is by far the most favourable method.

In-salon advertisement

You can do this by posting a vacancy in your window for passers-by to see or for the attention of clients, who are a great source of potential team members and who can tell their friends, etc. You can also let your staff know about possible job vacancies via the staff noticeboard and in staff meetings.

Salon website

If you have your own website, make sure you create a 'Recruitment' section where you can advertise vacancies. You may even leave permanent vacancies there for those positions you regularly find difficult to fill, so that you get an ongoing flow of CVs to consider.

Online

There are several recruitment sites online that are generic and cover all sectors. But advertising is not always free and can be expensive, so it is worth shopping around.

Specialist internet sites

There are several sites that specialise in the hair and beauty sector, or even just hair or beauty. Rates can be expensive, so negotiate!

Jobcentre

Your local jobcentre should advertise your vacancy free of charge (through the Jobcentre Plus website) and this can be a useful method of recruiting staff.

Local media

Your local paper will have a 'situations vacant' section for advertising, but remember to negotiate on terms. For instance, could they run an advert over several weeks for a discounted rate? Or what about getting free online advertising to go with their print media? (Remember that some local papers will have a web version, too).

Other salons

If you are on good, friendly terms with other salon managers, and enjoy a professional relationship with them, you can create a network. This means that if a CV comes in for a vacancy that you cannot fill, you can ask the candidate if you can pass it on to your contact (you must check with them first). This can be a reciprocal arrangement and you can work together if rivalry is not too intense or the other salon is not too close-by.

Training providers

If you are using a training provider, they may have a situations vacant website or noticeboard where you can advertise the position.

AD HOC APPLICATIONS

It is useful to have a company application form that you keep at reception for any impromptu would-be employees who may call in. It is helpful to give an applicant a form to fill in, asking for their details if they do not have a CV to hand or have popped in unprepared. Some younger recruits will not even have a CV yet, for instance, Saturday staff or school leavers; so it is good to have a form that requests some of the information that a CV would contain. Ad hoc applicants can be asked to fill it in there and then and hand it back to a receptionist, to pass on to you (or whoever you choose to handle your recruitment), with a timeframe given for when somebody will get back to them.

PROFESSIONAL COURTESY

Getting back to people is an essential part of the integrity you need to have to be a good manager – whether this is to clients who have complaints or issues, staff who need to speak to you or potential employees. It simply does not do on a professional level to be lax in responding by a certain time. If this is one of your less favourable character traits, try to develop systems to alleviate it. Whether the answer is favourable or unfavourable, people always should be given the courtesy of a response and should not have to chase for one. The only time I do not feel I have to get back to people is in response to cold-callers, or blanket generic emails sent out to all salon owners on a mailing list. Otherwise, make sure that you do respond. It may be to say that you cannot respond in full for a certain time period, but you should at least reply to let people know that you will be getting back to them at some point if you can, as an acknowledgement.

HOW TO READ A CV

A good CV should be no more than two pages long and should contain both professional work history and personal information. It should include a photograph, address, landline and mobile phone numbers, email address, details of qualifications, school information (exam results, name of school attended, etc), work history (starting at the most recent position and working backwards), current salary details and hobbies. It can also contain details of visas held, languages spoken, driving status (such as full driving licence) and other relevant information.

Warning bells...

These should be ringing if you notice any of the following:
- various changes in job roles (investigate each job change in detail)
- lots of different positions held for minimal time
- uncertainty – work being seen as a short-term option, such as long-term plans for travelling
- negative comments about previous employers
- lack of referees or disparity between number of jobs and lack of referees.

I would not advise interviewing a candidate if you see too many of the above on a first reading of a CV, unless you are looking for temporary cover. For long-term employees, you should be looking for the following:
- longevity in each position
- minimal number of positions held
- long periods of time working with a company where lots of natural, upwards progression is evident
- good references
- good earnings (particularly if pay is commission-related)
- positive comments about previous positions.

THE EMPLOYMENT PROCESS

Once you have sifted through CVs, you need to follow the recruitment procedure. This follows a particular pattern:
- shortlist potential candidates
- first interview
- second interview
- trade test
- trial day
- probationary period
- contract of employment.

This sounds like a lengthy process, but all the stages are equally important. Try to keep the time between the different stages short and snappy – it should not drag on too long or you might put off a possibly excellent employee with too much dilly-dallying.

If a candidate whose CV you like makes your shortlist, conduct a first interview as soon as possible. Successful applicants who pass this interview stage should then be followed-up quite quickly with a second interview. If the candidate is at senior level, I would also conduct a trade test at this stage.

Always ask the potential employee to bring in their one of their own models, then choose another yourself – another staff member is ideal, as they can assess their working practice and attitude for you.

For technicians, I would advise seeing at least two types of technical work – fine intricate foil highlights and a global (all over) colour, for instance. For hairdressers, I would ask for a restyle cut and an up-do (chignon) or a blow-dry. For therapists, I would ask to see some waxing and massage and, for manicurists, a French polish and pedicure with cuticle removal. You can choose which treatments you wish to see; but make them intricate. The candidate should wear or bring with them some sort of uniform if applicable (for example for beauty therapy).

The harder you make the recruitment procedure, the more you can learn about the candidates.

TRADE TESTS

Whoever is conducting the trade test, whether it is you or a senior member of the relevant team (head therapist, spa manager, technical manager, artistic director, head receptionist, and so on), they should remember that a trade test is not just to assess the intricacies of the treatment or service. Look at how well the candidate consults their client before treatment, and how well they interact with other team members, for example in asking where equipment is, and so on – your team will then get a 'feel' for the applicant. For the model you provide, get a debrief 'a productive team member' afterwards to analyse how well the treatment was performed, and ask the all-important question: would they go back to the candidate as a paying customer? If no, you have your answer.

TRIAL DAYS AND PROBATION

For junior team members, choose another trusted junior to 'buddy' up with the candidate on their trial day to see how well they integrate into the team and look after the customers.

For receptionists, the head receptionist or most senior receptionist, should also buddy-up and see how they cope with welcoming clients and giving general customer service. If they do not have industry experience, make sure they are at least assessed on how well they interact with clients and team members, and how they use all types of communication – even if they cannot make bookings or answer the phone.

You will never always make 100% the right decision, and nor will your interviewee; so it is wise to issue a probationary period – it is as much for them to see if they like you (your salon) as it is for you to see how you like them. Three to six months' probation is normal, and you can write this into your contract of employment so they are fully aware of the procedure from the beginning. Once the probation period has elapsed, you can conduct a first appraisal to assess how things are going.

INTERVIEWING

Make sure your interview is uninterrupted. You should not keep people waiting for more than 10 minutes and, personally, I would not bother with candidates who are more than 10 minutes late (without very good reason). Give the applicant an application form to fill in, even if they have a CV. Ask reception staff later about their manner and demeanour while they are waiting.

FIRST INTERVIEW

A first interview need not take more than 20 minutes. Try to create a semi-informal environment, where you are sitting close to each other but there is a desk to lean on; for example, at the end of the desk rather than with the desk between you. Make sure chairs are at the same height so you are communicating at eye level. After introducing yourself and stating your position, relax them at the start by asking them if they found the place easily and make small talk about travel. You could offer refreshments to the applicant, such as tea, coffee or water. You can then begin by asking the applicant what they know about the company and how they found out about it and the position. Failure to do their homework or carry out research on your brand will not create a favourable impression, so find out what they know about you and how much they really understand about your brand. Poor personal hygiene or scruffy appearance (at interview level) should obviously ring warning bells, since presentation is vital in our industry. Poor nonverbal communication will also be a negative indicator – you are looking for a candidate to maintain eye contact, show a keen interest in what you say and smile.

Then run through your history and offer a brief salon history (when you opened, how many staff you have, the type of clients you cater for, and so on) to give some background information on your company and fill in the gaps from their research. Describe the managerial structure and give them some core facts about the company and the position they are applying for.

A desk can act as a barrier in an interview, so try to minimise its effect.

TYPES OF QUESTIONS TO ASK

Open question

Who, why, when, what, how, tell me ... a question to which an applicant cannot answer yes or no and which requires more information in their response.

Closed question

Is, can, did, could, should, would ... a question to which an applicant can answer yes or no and which should only be used to clarify an answer.

Always used **open questions** in interview situations and only use **closed questions** to confirm information, eg *'Did you say earlier that you undertook training at that salon?'*

Open questions

You can ask the candidate some different open questions, such as the following:

- Tell me about yourself (a very general question).
- What made you want to be a hairdresser/ technician/therapist/ manicurist?
- What experience do you have that relates to the hair/beauty industry (or service industry)?
- Where do you currently go to have hair/beauty services and why do you go there?
- What did you notice about the salon while you were waiting at reception?
- What personality traits and qualities do you think are needed to make a good operator?
- What disadvantages are there in being a busy therapist/ hairdresser/manicurist?
- What defines or epitomises excellent customer service for you?
- Tell me about a good service experience you have had recently and a bad one.
- What makes you want to work here – what elements appeal to you?
- Do you work better in a team environment or on your own?
- What contribution do you think you would be making to the team?
- What motivates you?
- How would you deal with the following situation?
  (Think of a difficult client scenario to present here.)
- What do you consider to be your strengths/weaknesses?
- Tell me about your last position.
- What is the biggest compliment anybody ever paid you?
- What is your greatest achievement/ biggest mistake?
- What is the single thing that you most want me to remember about you?
- What would your last employer say about you if I contact them for a reference?
- Where do you see yourself in 10 years' time?

General questions

Much, of course, will depend on who you are interviewing and at what level their role will be. However, some general things I like asking are 'What were your observations on the salon while you were waiting for me?' This often becomes a very revealing insight into how much they want the job and how much notice they took of their surroundings.

Questions for receptionists

For receptionists, the questions need to be far more service-orientated, so include such things as:

- the advantages and disadvantages of working in a salon
- coping with stress
- working in the service industry
- their skill-set, strengths and weaknesses (memory, administration, numerical and organisational skills).

You should also cover some role-play scenarios (lost bookings, unhappy clients and so on).

Questions for senior team members

Some of these questions would be as unsuitable for a junior as they would be for a senior managerial position, but they create a good basis on which to come up with your own questions. Alternatively, after examining their work history in detail, use some of the following types of direct questions for more senior team members:

- What ancillary aspects of the job do you currently enjoy (such as training, magazine work, photographic work, education and so on)?
- What are the advantages to your career in moving to the salon?
- What do you perceive will be the advantages for your clientele?
- How many of your clients use link-services, eg beauty, technical, etc?
- What is your current price structure and salary structure?
- What was your previous earning potential and commission?
- What is your weekly turnover? (They should know this; if not, why not?)
- Why do you think you are a good 'people person'?
- Are there any services or treatments in the company's offering (check website or brochure) that you cannot offer?
- What is your current situation? Does your boss know you are attending interviews? Have you told them you are unhappy?

Listening carefully

Bear in mind that there are no right or wrong answers – you will have to develop a gut feel with an understanding that what makes one person special (bubbly, extrovert) need not be seen as a negative characteristic in another (we need introverts, too!). Interviewing is a managerial skill to perfect: remember that it is much more about listening than it is talking, so it is your chance to listen to the clues in what they are saying and assess them properly.

AT THE END

Make notes on their application form as you go then, after the applicant has left, score them out of 10. It may be that you decide not to pursue any further but may file for future reference, and your score(s) will help you remember how you assessed the candidate. Wrap up the interview by telling them when you will get back to them (give them a date), and how (phone call, email, etc), then escort them back to reception and shake their hand, thanking them for coming along.

Questions you cannot ask

Keep an open mind – appearances can be deceptive, although first impressions matter greatly.

Any questions relating to pregnancy or motherhood are illegal: you cannot discriminate against a candidate on the basis of their family situation. Likewise, a candidate's ethnic origin, sexuality or religion cannot be part of your selection criteria.

FOLLOW-UP AFTER INTERVIEW

Have a standard 'no thanks' letter that you can simply sign and send off to anyone who has paid you the courtesy of being interested in working for you. You do not need to respond to unsolicited CVs that you are sent, but anyone who you have seen at interview level (at whatever stage) should receive a letter or be emailed with a short note. Something along the following lines will suffice:

Interviewing is a managerial skill to perfect, and I have learned not to be too judgemental of people: keep an open mind.

> *Dear Ms X*
>
> *Thank you for attending your recent interview with Hellen's Hair & Beauty Salon. Unfortunately, your application was not successful at this time. Thank you for your kind interest in the position and, on behalf of the company, I would like to wish you every success in your future career.*
>
> *Yours sincerely*

You do not need to go into detail about what made their application unsuccessful or why. But a short letter is just plain good manners and prevents any negative feedback about your brand.

SECOND INTERVIEW

If you want to conduct a second interview, go to the next level and start the rebooking of the trade test within a week of the first interview; but you should give the applicant time to find a model, etc. In the second interview, you can be less generic and more detailed. For instance, you can ask questions about when they could start, possible salary, what their role might involve (run through the job description), how they could be proactive in building up a client base, what would be expected of them, etc.

Give candidates the opportunity to ask specific questions as well, and make sure they are not under any contractual obligations which may affect their future employment, such as a **radius clause**.

In this interview, it is prudent to go through more detail such as work stations, junior rotas, opening times, days off, training and education, uniform (if applicable). You should also include information about what happens next, with regard to trade tests and salary structures, etc. Explain when and how they will hear if they are successful and what will happen next.

Radius clause

A contractual clause which may prevent an employee from conducting services on their clients elsewhere within a stated period of time.

OFFER OF EMPLOYMENT

Once this stage is reached, you should send an offer of employment letter or email with the following details:

- job role/title
- start date
- salary package
- details of when the induction booklet, contract of employment and terms and conditions of employment will be issued
- uniform requirements
- hours of work
- days off
- number of days holiday
- probationary period
- a welcome to the company.

Give the applicant a timeframe by which to accept the offer and ask for confirmation either in writing or by email. Do not stop advertising the position until you have received the acceptance confirmation (and inform them of this fact).

COMMUNICATION STYLES AND TECHNIQUES

In order to be a good interviewer, you need to be a good communicator. This requires a certain level of self-awareness in order to recognise your own personal style of communicating and that of others. There are three basic styles of communication:

- aggressive
- passive
- assertive.

AGGRESSIVE COMMUNICATION

The aggressive style of communication normally indicates a poor listener who can be quite closed minded and has difficulty in seeing another person's point of view. The aggressive communicator often interrupts and monopolises the conversation and can be quite domineering and bossy, putting others down and never thinking they are wrong. They can be quite overpowering and impatient, are likely to have difficulty showing appreciation and can use bullying tactics, both in their verbal and nonverbal communication (shaking fists, etc) to get results. This style often fosters an atmosphere of defiance and resistance.

PASSIVE COMMUNICATION

The passive communicator generally does not like to make waves or disagree with others, avoiding confrontations where possible; consequently they can have difficulty in standing up for themselves. They often hesitate and do not speak up, appearing both apologetic and self-conscious with a lack of self-esteem, and may allow others to make decisions on their behalf. The passive communicator often 'sits on the fence' and does not get what they want, clamming up if they feel they are being treated unfairly, often complaining instead of taking action, or withdrawing further into themselves and feeling powerless about their situation.

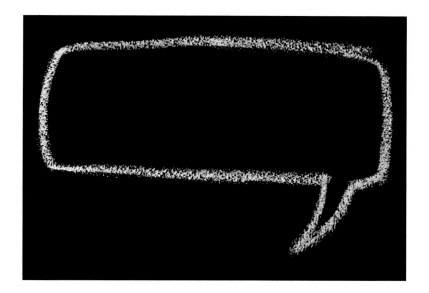

ASSERTIVE COMMUNICATION

The assertive communicator is an effective, active listener, who believes that they and others are valuable, without judgement or labelling. They express themselves directly and honestly, but also check on other people's feelings. They are confident and self-aware, open, flexible and proactive as well as being decisive. They tend to be action-orientated and firm, and demonstrate a fair and consistent style, using open, natural gestures and direct eye contact. They confront problems and do not allow negative feelings to build up, thriving on enthusiasm and positivity.

DIFFERENT STYLES

Few people completely use one or the other style of communication; most of us are a mixture of styles. For instance, the **passive-aggressive communicator** is fond of manipulation – avoiding direct confrontation (passive) but attempting to get results through devious behaviour (aggressive). This can result in the worst type of salon politics and rumour-mongering. Always try to analyse a potential employee's communication style and judge how well it will fit into your team. It will take all types to make up your staff – do not just be steered towards assertive communicators – but do take note of the personal styles of individuals, ready for personnel matters in the future.

Clearly, while the assertive style is the one to strive for, there are times when you will need to be aggressive (during emergencies), and other times when the passive style is called for (when emotions are running high or sensitivity is paramount). Being aware of your style and working on its negatives is a good principle for effective communication.

EFFECTIVE COMMUNICATION

Whatever your style, in order to communicate effectively it is important that you should:
• speak clearly and unambiguously
• vary your voice tone and inflections
• speak with courtesy and confidence
• use professional vocabulary (and not jargon)
• listen well (there is a reason why we have two ears and one mouth!).

COMMUNICATION TECHNIQUES

We all communicate all the time, but often without actually realising which communication techniques we are using.

Open and closed
Open communication takes place through discussion and involvement by both parties; closed communication is through passing on information without involving the recipient.

Formal and informal

Formal communication is a formatted, structured style (as used in formal letters and interview situations), whereas informal communication is an unofficial, 'through the grapevine' type of communication.

One- and two-way

One-way communication requires no answer (it can be someone giving out information) but two-way communication means a responsive feedback is required.

Vertical and horizontal

A vertical communication technique is when information is passed down from a high level; for example, managers communicating down the chain of command (manager to trainee, for example). Horizontal communication is the sharing of information among peers, or people along the same levels of responsibility (such as one department manager to another department manager).

Direct language

This might involve, for example, replacing 'I'll try' with 'I will'. 'we can't' with 'we can' is most effective. Avoid words like 'ok', 'sort of', 'do you know what I mean?', 'um' and 'ah'.

COMMUNICATION DELIVERY

These communication techniques can be delivered in three main ways:
- **verbal or oral** – spoken
- **nonverbal or visual communication** – through body language, gestures or facial expressions
- **written** – through letters, memos, emails, etc.

Visual communication

Visual, non-verbal communication is by far the most impactful way to get our message over. Statistics suggest that we retain 80% of information received visually, as opposed to only 5% of that received verbally. Therefore, demonstrating messages through visual media can have more impact, but consistent communication is a good mix of all three elements. Remember, it only takes a matter of seconds for a first impression to be formed.

Effective communication is therefore a combination of these three types:
- **55% visual/body language**
- **38% vocal/tone of voice**
- **7% verbal/word**

Positive body language can include smiling, eye contact, open palms, a respectful personal distance, and open body posture.

INDUCTION PROGRAMMES

An induction programme for new staff involves several elements and it is worth spending time getting it right.

STAFF HANDBOOK

It is a good idea to produce a short handbook or booklet which briefs a potential employee on how the salon runs and gives general information about the day-to-day things that will affect their job. This does not replace the full terms and conditions of employment, or the contract of employment, but can give a helpful brief overview. The basis of this should be a summary of:
- the salon's standards
- how you wish the salon to run
- your expectations of the employee.

You could include:
- company mission statement or brand ethos
- customer care and client relations – the 'chair-side or couch-side manner' you wish to adopt
- appointment/booking procedures
- staff conduct
- confidentiality matters
- stock control
- health and safety matters
- opening hours and times and what your requirements are (such as to arrive 15 minutes before to prepare for the first client)
- appearance requirements (uniform/dress code)
- sickness procedure (who to call, by when, etc)
- holiday procedure (how to book holiday, etc)
- details of their supervisor
- treatment rooms/work areas
- other salon policies – smoking, etc.

An induction booklet can be given to a potential employee at second interview stage, before a final offer of employment is made, so they are fully aware of your expectations, even before they start working for you.

BUDDY SYSTEM

Once new employees start work with you, their induction programme involves making sure that any training or education required is carried out at the start. It normally works best to create a buddy system for new employees, so an existing employee can help 'show them the ropes', and their immediate supervisor can 'mentor' them during their probationary period. They should go through the information needed to start performing their duties over a period of weeks and get them up to speed with the salon's policies and procedures. Longer-term training and education may take place after the probationary period has been successfully passed.

What induction should cover

During their induction period, the following matters should be covered through in-salon coaching and supervision:
- company history
- staff profiles, roles and responsibilities
- product and treatment ranges used
- health and safety procedures
- client confidentiality
- job role and description in detail
- salon policies and procedures
- reporting lines
- HR elements (terms and conditions).

JOB DESCRIPTIONS

To get the best out of our team members, we need to make sure they have a thorough understanding of the role that their job entails. The best way to do this is to produce a brief (one page is fine) job description. You can keep it quite generic, but be sure to note what you expect in the following areas.

GENERAL REQUIREMENTS

These requirements will include the following:
- attendance
- appearance
- customer service
- work environment (such as room, work station, cleanliness, tidiness)
- communication – with whom and how
- grievances – reporting lines to their supervisor
- training/after-hours commitments (meetings, etc).

TECHNICAL REQUIREMENTS

Technical requirements will include the following:
- diligence and conscientiousness in performing tasks
- KPIs – what they are and how they will be tracked (refer to Book 2 Chapter 3 for more information on KPIs)
- client consultations and analysis procedures
- communication procedures with other team members
- attitude
- product usage.

DIFFERENT JOB DESCRIPTIONS

It is important to tailor the job description to suit the operator. I would advise you to have a different job description for each role in the salon, so you should cover the following:
- salon manager (if not you!)
- assistant manager or deputy manager
- technical director (colour)
- artistic director (hair)
- creative directors (artistic team members)
- senior stylists
- stylist
- graduate stylist
- apprentice
- head apprentice/head junior
- head/senior receptionist
- receptionist
- beauty/spa director
- senior therapist
- therapist
- nail technician
- office/admin/PA.

Job description – stylist

General
- To ensure the department is clean and tidy and suitable for clients to receive services.
- To provide your own high quality cutting and styling equipment or any such equipment that is not provided by the company.
- To always inform reception if you are away from your work station or staff area and to keep them informed of your whereabouts at all times.
- To look groomed – with freshly washed hair and newly applied make-up at all times.

- To be immaculately dressed in clean, pressed clothes at all times.
- To arrive for work 15 minutes before your start time to prepare for your working day.
- To clean and tidy your work station during your working day and at the end of your working day, including your lockable area.
- To attend any meetings/training sessions or courses with reasonable notice at times which may differ from your normal working hours.

Performing technical services

- To perform excellent and thorough hairdressing services at all times in a diligent and conscientious manner.
- To retain new clients and existing clients alike through achieving excellent technical results and by providing outstanding customer service levels.
- To perform a thorough and detailed consultation on each client you are given, creating a plan of future treatment.
- To analyse fully each client's hair and scalp, texture, density, skin tone, face shape and condition and recommend the relevant in-salon treatment and home care.
- To analyse the client's needs and establish their service and visit expectations.
- To meet and exceed those expectations.
- To deliver exceptional customer service at all times.
- To create a plan of on-going treatment bespoke to the customer.
- To ensure, to the best of your ability, that the client will re-book an appointment with you.
- To liaise with the technical and beauty team in helping to generate business for each other by word of mouth.
- To introduce yourself to the clients of your colleagues and recommend the relevant technical services.
- To liaise in the correct manner with reception (ie issuing your bills and charges and informing them of your time-keeping.)
- To liaise correctly with the technical team as per the Company Policy – ie calling the technician before they commence work and re-visiting the client afterwards to assess the finished result, informing the relevant operator of your time-keeping.
- To project a positive, motivated and enthusiastic manner to clients and staff alike.
- To use products by directed by your supervisor at all times unless for specific reasons or for specific clients.

Job description – beauty therapist/manicurist

General

- To ensure the department (your room and working area) is clean and tidy and suitable for clients to receive services.
- To adhere to the Beauty area cleaning rota as issued by your supervisor.
- To provide your own top quality personal equipment such as tweezers, clippers, etc. or any such equipment that is not provided by the company.
- To always inform reception if you are away from your treatment room/work station or staff area and to inform them of your whereabouts at all times.
- To look groomed – with freshly washed hair, clean and filed nails and newly applied make-up at all times.
- To be immaculately dressed in clean, pressed uniform (wearing the correct shoes) at all times.
- To arrive for work 15 minutes before your start time.
- To clean and tidy your treatment room/ work station during your working day and at the end of your working day, including your lockable area.
- To attend any meetings/training sessions or courses with reasonable notice at times.

Performing technical services

- To perform excellent and thorough services at all times in a diligent and conscientious manner.
- To retain new clients and existing clients alike through achieving excellent results and by providing outstanding customer service levels.
- To perform a thorough and detailed consultation on each client you are given.
- To analyse fully each client's skin texture, tone and condition nail condition, treatment contra-indications and lifestyle regime and recommend the relevant in-salon treatment and home care.
- To analyse the client's needs and establish their service and visit expectations.
  - To meet and exceed those expectations
  - To deliver exceptional customer service at all times
  - To create a plan of on-going treatment bespoke to the customer
  - To ensure, to the best of your ability, that the client will re-book an appointment with you
- To liaise with the technical and hairdressing teams in helping to generate business for each other by word of mouth.

- To introduce yourself to the clients of your colleagues in other teams and recommend the relevant services, liaising with them over your scheduling of appointments when working dually on clients.
- To liaise in the correct manner with reception (ie issuing your bills and charges and informing them of your time-keeping.)
- To complete the relevant record cards, customer liability forms and any other information as instructed by your Supervisor.
- To project a positive, motivated and enthusiastic manner to clients and staff alike.
- To use products as directed by your supervisor at all times unless for specific reasons or for specific clients.

SUMMARY

Attracting good team members is essential to our progress, and making sure we handle our recruitment in a professional manner is vital to our business reputations. A professional salon will rarely need to recruit key roles from the outside, but long-term reputations like this are built on good practice in our HR. We must make sure we gain a reputation for being selective and professional in our choice of team members and this must be echoed by the process we choose to select them.

Never be afraid to ask anyone, however experienced, to undergo a trade test. If they are truly professional, they will understand how vital it is to ensure they have the practical skills to be allowed to conduct services on paying customers. While our industry remains unregulated, it is non-negotiable that you, as a manager or owner, have a responsibility to have made sure their technical capabilities were sufficient for the role you are employing them to conduct.

Recruiting new employees is a skill which you will refine and improve during your management career. Do not be afraid to take up references and trade test but, most importantly, learn to be guided by your gut instinct; you will come to rely on it the longer you hold a responsible role.

Practise being an effective communicator – developing this skill will be invaluable for the plethora of activities the salon manager has to undertake.

CHAPTER 2
EMPLOYMENT OBLIGATIONS

This chapter covers what you need to know in order to employ staff. We will look at contracts of employment and the clauses you need to protect you and your employees. Also we'll cover how to manage your payroll, the legalities of commission-related pay and how to get to grips with legislation such as the Working Time Directive, the National Minimum Wage, and maternity pay and parental leave. We will also cover annual leave – how to manage your staff holidays and the pay implications involved.

RIGHTS AND OBLIGATIONS

By its very nature, employing people is a big responsibility. As salon owners and managers, it is assumed that you will have an understanding of how to implement any employment matters professionally and will be fully up to speed with changes in employment obligations. There are several complex areas to get to grips with; it is important to have a good basic knowledge of all of them.

EMPLOYEE RIGHTS

Employees have several different rights that are based in law. The most important of these are as follows:
- to be given an itemised pay slip
- not to be unfairly dismissed
- to receive written reasons for dismissal
- to receive and provide a minimum period of notice
- to receive statutory maternity pay and maternity leave
- to receive statutory sickness pay
- to have a statement of particulars of employment.

Employers have obligations to their employees. They must:
- pay their employees (as long as they are available for work), even if there is no work for them; employers cannot pick and choose the days on which there is work to do
- ensure their employees are safe while doing their jobs, and provide specialist equipment, if required, at no expense to the employee
- refund employees for any expenses incurred at or during work
- act in a reasonable manner towards their employees, with mutual trust and understanding.

EMPLOYEE OBLIGATIONS

Employees have obligations, too. They must:
- devote their time during the working day to the employer's business; this time must not be used to pursue their own interests
- not divulge any confidential information relating to their employer's business to others
- not disclose details of intellectual property that belongs to their employer; this remains their employer's property
- do their job diligently and properly
- be honest with their employment; workers must not profit at their employer's expense
- obey reasonable instructions during their employment; and carry out the job they were employed to do.

EMPLOYER'S FINANCIAL OBLIGATIONS

There are several financial obligations that you have to fulfil when you employ someone. Your book-keeper or accountant can carry these out on your behalf, or you can learn to do it yourself. An employer must:

- deduct the correct amount of **PAYE** from the employee's pay
- work out how much **NICs** you and the employee have to pay
- keep accurate records of your employees' pay and the PAYE and NICs due
- make payments to **HMRC** every month, or quarter (if PAYE and NICs amount to less than £600 per month).

Year-end responsibilities

At the end of the tax year an employer must:

- send a return to the tax office showing the details of each employee's total pay and PAYE and NICs due
- send details to the tax office of certain expenses they have paid to employees or benefits they have provided to them (P11D)
- give each employee who has paid PAYE and NICs and is still working for them at the end of the tax year a certificate of their pay, PAYE and NICs details (P60).

CONTRACTS OF EMPLOYMENT

There is no legal requirement under English law that states there should be a written contract of employment, at the time of writing. However, under the Employment Rights Act 1996, employers must provide their employees with a statement in writing of certain details of their employment within two months of their starting employment.

WRITTEN STATEMENT

Details that must be included in the written statement are:

- the name of the employee and the name of the employer
- the date on which the employment commenced
- the date on which the employee's continuous employment began, taking into account any employment with a previous employer which counts toward that period
- the rate of pay or the method of calculating gross pay in a specified period
- the length of interval between pay periods
- the normal hours of work and terms and conditions applying to those working hours, and if enhanced payments are made for overtime or shift working, details of those enhancements
- the terms relating to the entitlement of holiday pay and pay for public holidays, together with details of how the monetary value will be calculated or accrued

PAYE

(Pay As You Earn) The system of withholding income tax from each payment made by the employer – it must be remitted promptly to the government.

NICs

(National Insurance Contributions) These come out of an employee's pay and build up their entitlement to certain state benefits, including the State Pension. Refer to Book 1 Chapter 3 for more detail.

HMRC

(Her Majesty's Revenue and Customs) The government organisation responsible for collecting tax.

You can find the P11D and P60 at the HMRC website

- the terms and conditions relating to any pay during periods of sickness or injury, or a note as to where these details may be found
- the terms and conditions relating to any membership of any pension scheme administered by the company or made available to employees, or a note of where these details may be found
- the length of notice the employee must give to the employer or the employer must give to the employee to terminate the employment
- the title of the job or a brief description of the work the employee is to do
- whether or not the employment is permanent and, if not, the expected duration of the contract of employment or, for a fixed term contract, the termination date
- the place of work or, if the employee has no fixed place of work, and indication of this fact and the address of the employer
- any collective agreements directly affecting the terms and conditions of employment, or a note as to where these details may be found
- for employees required to work outside the UK for periods greater than one month, details of the terms of their employment while abroad and on their return to the UK
- details about the disciplinary rules applicable to the employee and the grievance procedure or a reference to where these may be found
- a statement as to whether the employer holds a contracting-out certificate in relation to any pension scheme operated by the employer.

STATUTORY MINIMUM REQUIREMENTS

If you are a member of a trade body, such as the NHF (National Hairdressers, Federation) or FHT (Federation of Holistic Therapists), you can use their standard contract template. However, if you want to write your own, make sure you include the following information, and detail each point as listed above, to ensure you are providing the correct information:

- name
- date (continuous) employment started
- pay and intervals of pay
- hours of work
- holiday entitlement (how many days per year – pro rata, etc)
- sickness and sick pay (SSP)
- pension and pension schemes
- notice period (by either party)
- job title and brief description of duties
- duration of (if) fixed-term contract

- place of work
- trade union agreements
- whether or not required to work outside UK
- disciplinary procedure
- grievance procedure
- rights of suspension
- post-employment obligations (such as non-solicitation).

NOTICE PERIODS

An employer is required to give at least the following periods of notice to an employee:
- one month to less than two years' employment – one week
- two years' employment – two weeks
- one additional week for each further whole year's employment at the date the notice period expires, up to a maximum of twelve weeks' notice in total.

If the employee has been continuously employed for more than one month, he or she is required to give the employer no less than one week's notice to terminate the employment contract. If the employment contract does not specify the lengths of notice periods, a court would consider the duties performed by the employee and decide what a reasonable notice period should be. For instance, for a director of a medium-sized company, the notice period could be six months.

This does not mean that your employees are required to give the same notice to you should they decide to leave as you need to give them; you have the right to one week's notice as an employer.

If, under her/his contract, the notice that an employee has to give her/his employer exceeds the statutory minimum notice the employer is entitled to receive, this will take precedence over the statutory minimum.

Payment in lieu of notice

In the nature of our business, if salon employees operating a clientele decide to leave, this minimal notice period is beneficial, as serving longer notices (if the employee offers) may be detrimental to the business if there is any risk that clients may leave to follow them. You can even consider payment in lieu of notice if you are nervous about them working out their notice period and the risk this could pose to your business.

CONFIDENTIALITY, NON-SOLICITATION AND RADIUS CLAUSES

There are many urban myths about these elements of salon employees' contracts, but all of these clauses are particularly relevant to our industry and in others where client relationships are an intrinsic part of the success of the business, for instance, the legal profession.

Confidentiality clauses

These refer to the information that employees may have access to in the course of carrying out their day-to-day duties, which is deemed to be confidential and wholly the property of the company. This may include handling personal information (under the Data Protection Act) which has been given exclusively to the company by the customer and is the company's property, or any other lists, data, records or information (including names, addresses and telephone numbers of customers, as well as their personal technical/service data) which is deemed to be confidential. This remains the company's property and taking this information without your consent can be considered theft by the employee. This information may also include business plans, financial information, marketing, sales and other such information which is deemed to be confidential.

Radius clauses

These can offer you some protection regarding losing staff to other rival businesses. They will only remain in force for the length of the employee's post-employment obligations as defined in the terms and conditions of their employment and their contract of employment (ie 6 months). There is an urban myth that they are not valid or do not hold up in court. As with anything legal, there have been a number of cases over the years where they have been upheld successfully, and also a number where they have not offered the protection sought. As always, each case will have its own particular circumstances.

Validity of radius clauses

However, their validity will probably be dependent on a few factors: for example, how the clause was worded (so a two-mile radius in central London that denied the employee the opportunity to work in most potential salons may be considered too stringent – the court cannot rule in favour of any employment law that restricts a person from being able to earn a reasonable living), or how long post-employment the clause should remain in force for (a reasonable length of time).

It is worth remembering, however, that the radius clause should not restrict the employee from working in a salon within the geographical area (and therefore limiting their ability to earn money through gainful employment), merely from working on clients that belong to the salon within the zone. In other words (and everything will depend on how the clause is worded), the employee could get a job in another local salon within the radius, but would not be permitted to carry out the services for which they were employed by your salon on customers that are defined as belonging to your salon, whether they actually solicit them or not. So, even if the client follows them of their own free will, if your clause is worded correctly, you may find that the employee will be in breach of contract if they carry out any of the 'services' as defined in their contract. If their new place of work has enough new clients to furnish them with, their ability to earn is therefore undiminished.

As is the case with much of our legislation, there are always new 'test' cases that are becoming benchmark legal scenarios. It is therefore important to keep yourself up to date with what is happening that particularly concerns our industry through the trade press or by joining associations like the NHF or BABTAC.

Non solicitation clauses

A non-solicitation clause is perhaps the most important aspect of any contract in our profession, as it prevents the employee from soliciting any clients that belong to the salon. A non-solicitation clause will state that the employee cannot attempt to 'solicit' any business of the salon, ie they cannot contact a client when no longer in your employ who is deemed to be a customer of the salon (originally). Therefore, if they move to a rival salon, they should not be able to let salon customers know (whether verbally, in writing or in any other media, such as by text or using the internet) where they are. Unless you have a stringent radius clause in place, if the client leaves the salon and naturally finds the operator it is their freedom of choice as to whether they choose to go with them to their new place of work (even if they go there on a different basis, for example self-employed contractor).

If a busy stylist or therapist comes to you with a clientele, it is vital to list by name, as an appendix to your contract, which clients are deemed to be those belonging to the company, and which have been brought with them upon joining the salon. This solves any possible dispute later on about who they can contact, and who they are not allowed to get in touch with if things do not work out or they choose to move on.

TAKING LEGAL ADVICE

I would always suggest you take proper legal advice in establishing your non-solicitation and radius clauses, but you can download my example at www.ultimatesalonmanagement.com. It is very important to ensure that you and your employee fully understand these elements of the contract, as taking phone numbers and subsequently contacting clients or working within a defined radius may also have implications under the Data Protection Act for you and for them, as well as breaching any clauses concerning theft of company property. Remember, there is a time limit to these post-employment obligations within which the employee has to comply.

MANAGING YOUR PAYROLL

You may choose to manage your payroll in-house, or you may decide to use the services of a book-keeper or accountant to help you. Personally, I would suggest that, particularly if the time you can devote to your managerial duties is limited, your office hours can be spent more wisely monitoring and managing your turnover, income and expenses so you can directly impact the business, rather than working out pay slips; but it is your preference.

PAYROLL TERMS

The following are some terms you will need to be familiar with.

P45

This is a statement which relates to each employee detailing their tax code, NI number and other personal data.

P11 and P11D

A P11 is a sheet detailing the salary paid and deductions made for each employee.

The P11D is a statement of bonuses and extra possible taxable income given annually to the employee.

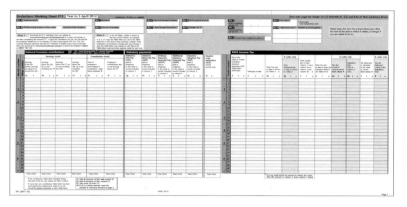

To view full size version visit the HMRC website.

Tax code

This refers to the taxable allowance calculated for the particular individual, issued by HMRC.

Tax reference number

This is the reference of the employer's tax office to which payments are made and where queries are dealt with.

P35

This is an employer's annual return showing the details of all employees' PAYE and NICs collectively.

P14

This is an end-of-year summary used for each employee to record the totals from the form P11.

Pay adjustment tables

These are the tables and systems used for working out free-of-tax pay and allowances for employees.

Taxable pay tables

These are used in conjunction with pay adjustment tables to work out the tax due from taxable pay.

LEGISLATION

WORKING TIME REGULATIONS 1998

The Working Time Regulations apply to all workers and specify maximum weekly worked hours, rest periods during the working day and minimum rest periods between working days and conditions for night shift workers. The entitlements may be excluded or modified by individual written agreements, collective agreements or workforce agreements.

Current legislation states that no employee may work more than an average of 48 hours per week, including overtime. This hourly average should be calculated over a 17-week period. There are some areas that you need to clarify with regard to what constitutes work, and what does not. So:

- not work – is being on call, travelling to your job, being at lunch, taking work home of your own accord (not part of a working arrangement)
- work – is driving as part of a job, being at a working breakfast or lunch.

TIME ON CALL

A case in the European Court of Justice (ECJ) ruled that time spent 'on call' (or standby) has to be counted entirely as working time if the employee is required to be physically present at her/his place of work, or another place determined by the employer and to be available for work. This is the case even if the worker is resting. However, if the worker is merely required to be contactable, but does not need to be physically present at a particular place determined by the employer unless called in, that period of on-call duty is not counted as working time.

COMPULSORY REST PERIODS

An employee is entitled to a rest period of 11 consecutive hours between each working day, and an uninterrupted rest period of no less than 24 hours in each seven-day period. This may be averaged out over two weeks, for instance a worker is hence entitled to two days' consecutive rest within a fortnight.

A worker is entitled to an uninterrupted break each working day of at least 20 minutes and this cannot be taken at the beginning or the end of the working day.

Young workers

Adolescent workers (between school-leaving age and under 18 years of age) have additional rights:

- each day they must have at least 12 hours' uninterrupted rest in every 24-hour period
- each week they must have two days (48 hours) of rest (this can be adjusted where it is justified for technical or organisational reasons)
- the averaging of hours for weekly work periods, applicable to adult workers, may not be used
- a rest period of at least 30 minutes when the working day is more than four and a half hours long
- a young person over compulsory school-leaving age and under 18 must not work more than eight hours per day and must not work more than 40 hours per week.

STATUTORY REDUNDANCY PAY

Under the Employment Rights Act 1996, an employee with more than two years' continuous service is entitled to redundancy pay if the employment is terminated because either the employer ceases business in the place where the employee is employed, or the needs of the business for work of the kind performed by the employee have diminished. Statutory redundancy pay is based on the age, average weekly earnings and length of continuous service of the employee. Average weekly earnings are capped at £400 (from 1 February 2011) and the length of service is capped at 20 years in calculating redundancy pay. For service performed while the employee was aged between 21 and 41, the employee is entitled to one week's pay for each complete year of employment, and for service performed over the age of 42, the employee is entitled to one and a half weeks' pay. The maximum statutory redundancy pay is £7200.00. The employee is entitled to 0.5 week's pay for each complete year of employment before the employee's 22nd birthday. There is no upper age limit on claiming statutory redundancy pay.

STATUTORY SICK PAY

After three months of continuous employment, employers must pay Statutory Sick Pay (SSP) to employees unable to work during sickness or injury for four days or more (the employee is not paid for the first three days of absence). Provided that the employee's gross earnings exceed £102 per week and eligibility provisions are satisfied, the rate of SSP is £81.60 per week from 6 April 2011. All employers are entitled to offset SSP payments against their National Insurance Contributions under the Percentage Threshold rules, which mean that very small employers receive relief for most, if not all of the SSP they have to pay.

EQUAL OPPORTUNITIES

Employers must not discriminate against employees because of their race, sex, marital status or disabilities. The employer's duties are set out in the Equal Pay Act 1970, Sex Discrimination Act 1975, Race Relations Act 1976, Disability Discrimination Act 1995, Part Time (Prevention of less Favourable Treatment) Regulations 2000 and European Fixed-Term Workers Directive. Further measures to prevent age, sexual orientation and religious discrimination are due to appear in the coming years.

NATIONAL MINIMUM WAGE

The National Minimum Wage (NMW) was introduced in 1999 and set out minimum hourly rates of pay dependent on the age of employees. Current NMW rates (at the time of writing) are as follows (not including tips or gratuities):

- apprentice rate, for apprentices under 19 or 19 or over and in the first year of their apprenticeship – £2.60 per hour gross pay
- ages between 16–17 years – £3.68 per hour gross pay
- ages between 18–21 years – £4.98 per hour gross pay
- over 21 years old – £6.08 per hour gross pay.

It is important to check for budgetary changes on rates.

There are exemptions to these rules which are applicable to those on training programmes, such as apprenticeships. The different rates that apply are as follows:

	Minimum wage	exemption
Age 16	exempt	exempt
Age 17	exempt	exempt
Age 18	£3.00 per hour	2
19 – 21	£3.00 per hour	2
22 – 25	£3.60 per hour	2 or 3
26+	3.60 per hour	none apply

Exemption 1: If trainees are under a contract or apprenticeship or modern apprenticeship they are exempt.

Exemption 2: If trainees are apprentices in their first year they will be exempt in that year only.

Exemption 3: If trainees are apprentices in their first year they will be exempt in that year only, but if they are doing accredited training and they are within the first six months of their employment you must pay them £3.20 per hour for that six-month period.

MATERNITY PAY

Under the Employment Rights Act 1996, the Employment Relations Act 1999 and the Maternity and Parental Leave Regulations, female employees are entitled (with no minimum service periods) to:
- paid time off to receive antenatal care
- protection from dismissal by reason of pregnancy or childbirth
- ordinary maternity leave of up to 18 weeks
- compulsory maternity leave whereby a woman is not allowed to return to work within two weeks of giving birth
- the right to return to work after ordinary maternity leave.

If the employee has 26 weeks of continuous service with an employer by 15 weeks before the expected week of childbirth, she is entitled to Statutory Maternity Pay (SMP). Subject to her average earnings exceeding £102 per week, SMP is payable for 18 weeks. The first six weeks of SMP is payable at 90% of the employee's normal weekly earnings over the eight-week period prior to the 14th week before confinement, and at £62.20 per week for the remaining 12 weeks. If the employee has at least one year's service by the 11th week before her expected confinement, she is entitled to additional maternity leave which starts at the end of her ordinary maternity leave and lasts for 29 weeks, commencing with the week of childbirth. If an employee is on additional maternity leave she has a right to return to work. However, she will lose this right if she does not reply within three weeks of her employer writing to ask her to confirm the date of the child's birth and whether she wants to return to work.

For up-to-date details of entitlements and conditions, check the money, tax and benefits pages of the Directgov website.

PATERNITY LEAVE/PARENTAL LEAVE

Parents, including parents of adopted children, with one year's service or more are entitled not to be reasonably refused up to 13 weeks' paid parental leave to care for a child within five years of the child's birth or adoption, provided the child was born or adopted after 15 December 1999. Various conditions apply to the taking of parental leave. Parents taking parental leave are protected from receiving detrimental treatment or dismissal because of the parental leave.

Eligibility

Parents must also be given the right to apply for flexible working hours, but to be eligible the employee must:

- have a child under the age of 17 or under 18 in the case of a disabled child
- have worked continuously with the employer for 26 weeks on the date the application was made
- make the application no later than two weeks before the child's 17th birthday or 18th birthday for the disabled child
- have responsibility for the child's upbringing
- be making the application to enable them to care for the child (not for any other reason)
- not be an agency worker
- not be a member of the armed forces
- not have made another application for flexible working hours under the right of this act during the past 12 months with the same employer.

DOMESTIC EMERGENCIES

Employees are entitled to take a reasonable amount of unpaid time off work for the purpose of looking after or making arrangements for a sick or injured dependant or to cope with the death of a dependant, etc.

HOLIDAY PAY

A worker is entitled to at least 5.6 weeks paid annual leave (equivalent to 28 days including bank holidays for those who work 5 days per week). The calculator for this can be found on www.businesslink.gov.uk.

Under the Working Time Regulations, employees with more than 13 weeks' service are entitled to four weeks' paid leave per year. Under the regulations, holiday pay entitlements cannot be carried forward into the next year and holiday may not be replaced by payments in lieu (you can decide to do this if you wish, but it is not a requirement). Most companies do not include public or bank holidays within the 20 day entitlement and they are treated as additional paid time off. If these fall within a normal day off then a day off in lieu should be given to the employee to take within the holiday year.

To calculate an individual's yearly holiday entitlement, multiply the number of days they work per week by 4.

So, if an employee is full-time and works five days per week for you, then 5 x 4 = an entitlement of 20 days over the full holiday year. If an employee works two days per week for you, then 2 x 4 = an entitlement of eight days over the full holiday year, etc, so calculate it on a pro-rata basis, depending on the number of days usually worked per week.

Points to note

There are several matters to clarify.

You need to set out in your terms and conditions or contract of employment when your holiday year runs. For instance, you can run your holiday year from April to end March, and the four weeks' holiday must be taken during this time. Alternatively you could use the calendar year, from January to December, or run it concurrent with your financial year.

You must state how holiday pay is accrued. Up until the holiday year starts, you can work out how many days are accrued up until the full holiday entitlement of four weeks begins on a pro-rata basis, ie 1.66 days paid holiday per month worked for full-time employees working five days per week.

You should also state how many consecutive weeks' holiday staff are allowed to take (for example, a maximum of three weeks at any one time), and what your salon policy is with regard to unpaid holidays (for sabbaticals or for people who wish to go travelling) – how much time is allowed, if any.

You should have a policy for the booking procedure for leave, for example if it should be booked at least six weeks in advance, on a first come, first served basis, etc. It is advisable to track this with a holiday application form to file in the employee's staff file, for future reference.

Holiday pay must be calculated at a rate equal to the average income over the previous 12 weeks, so commission-related pay must be considered when paying any holiday entitlement.

UNFAIR DISMISSAL

All employees with a minimum of one year's continuous service (however many days per week they work, so includes part-time or Saturday staff) have the right not to be unfairly dismissed. Unfair dismissal includes dismissal without good reason, constructive dismissal or dismissal following an unfair procedure.

An employee who believes his or her dismissal was unfair may bring a claim before an employment tribunal. Employment tribunals can make the employer unfairly dismissing the employee pay a basic award equivalent to the statutory redundancy pay the employee would have received had he/she been made redundant, and a compensatory award up to £68,400 from February 2011.

CONSTRUCTIVE DISMISSAL

This is deemed to be unfair dismissal that has been 'constructed' out of facts, or contrived, for example to make a case for dismissal where none really applies or breaching any mutual trust through demotion or harassment.

Constructive dismissal occurs when an employee leaves her/his employment because action taken by the employer amounts to a fundamental breach of contract and makes it difficult or impossible for the employee to continue working for that employer.

(Source: www.tradeangles.fsbusiness.co.uk)

SUMMARY

Employment obligations are not a choice – they are a continually evolving area of legislation that, as employers or salon managers, we are expected to know about. Legislation is ever-changing, and the onus is on employers to keep up to date with the latest information – the information contained in this chapter was correct at the time of going to print. If unsure, check the employment/employee pages of the Directgov website.

It is wise to remember that you, as an employer, need to protect your business as much as possible so ensure you have the correct post-employment obligations in force via your contract and terms and conditions of employment.

Feigning lack of knowledge regarding your responsibilities is not a good enough excuse, so if you are using a book-keeper or accountant to help you pay your team, you may be able to get advice on these other matters. Alternatively, search the internet or your trade body's websites to keep yourself informed. Many changes are put forward each year in the Chancellor's budget; so make sure you are up to date on budgetary changes as they happen.

CHAPTER 3
TRAINING AND DEVELOPMENT

This chapter will look at how your team can evolve through ongoing training and development. We will discuss the ways in which teams learn, as well as the different routes they can take to qualify for a career in the industry. We will cover what skills you need to develop to be a great trainer, and what you need to think about when devising your training programme. We will also consider the further education that is available to you and your teams, and how to manage change as your team progresses and develops.

THE IMPORTANCE OF TRAINING

Education is our most precious resource and is not a box that can ever be fully ticked. There should be a continuous programme of development for all team members, including managers. We never stop learning and regular training sessions – either in or out of the salon – help people to discover and develop new techniques and experiment with new innovations in our fields. Helping to map the future of our team members is an increasingly important element of our work. Empowering them to use every opportunity to learn and develop their skills is essential in order to retain them and keep them feeling inspired and motivated. By using our own skills to help our teams develop, we are investing in others and securing our own future success.

I would suggest that being an excellent hairdresser, colourist, therapist or nail technician is only 50% due to technical skill. The other 50% is undoubtedly down to being a great communicator, so it is wise to concentrate as much on teaching communication skills as on teaching practical and creative skills and product knowledge.

ENTRY ROUTES INTO THE INDUSTRY

Unregulated

This means that our industry is not controlled by a governing body.

There are different ways to train to become a fully qualified hairdresser, barber, beauty therapist or nail technician, which we need to be fully familiar with for our salon recruitment. Because our industry is **unregulated**, the quality of training can vary greatly, so trade testing is essential.

HAIRDRESSING AND BARBERING

APPRENTICESHIPS

NVQ

The acronym stands for National Vocational Qualification.

The most common type of training in hairdressing and barbering is through an apprenticeship. Apprenticeships involve training in the workplace and gaining a qualification at the end of that training. The technical qualifications gained during apprenticeships are the **NVQ** level 2 and 3 Diplomas. These qualifications make up the core parts of the following apprenticeship programmes.

Candidates with an NVQ should be job-ready as they have developed and trained on the job.

An apprenticeship will take between 2 – 5 years to complete, depending on the salon and level of training. Training may be entirely done vocationally (on the job), and may involve regular practical sessions or 'model nights' when the trainee gets a chance to put into practice the skills they have been observing during the course of their working days, which are spent assisting stylists, shampooing and generally helping out on the salon floor.

An apprenticeship is recognised as a great way to learn to become a hairdresser, as the experience gleaned from watching and learning on the salon floor is unique and very valuable to future employers. Years ago, apprenticeships were paid for, now we pay our apprentices on the job whilst they are learning. A hairdresser who has studied under an apprenticeship, particularly at a reputable salon, will already have developed customer service skills and a level of knowledge that may well surpass other training routes. Some salons get government funding through running a Modern Apprenticeship and others fund the learner's education themselves with a view to them working their way up through the salon ranks and eventually qualifying as a fully fledged hairdresser, therefore investing in their salon's futures. Depending on their age, the trainee may be subject to the minimum wage, and may or may not qualify for funding either by the training provider or direct to the employer.

The intermediate and advanced apprenticeships consist of the following elements.

Diploma in hairdressing or barbering
NVQ level 2 or 3 Diploma in hairdressing or barbering is the technical part of the qualification. It includes the practical skills and knowledge requirements needed to work in a salon environment.

Functional skills
Functional or key skills focus on developing the basic skills a learner will need in English and maths.

ERR
This part of the apprenticeship incorporates the Employee's Rights and Responsibilities, which are key to working in the industry.

PLTS
Personal Learning and Thinking Skills have been added to the apprenticeship package recently to ensure the learner has a clear understanding of what they do and why.

The intermediate apprenticeship is a great place to start training within the hairdressing industry as it allows the learners to develop intermediate skills. The advanced apprenticeship allows the learner to progress and develop more creative and advanced techniques. The experience gleaned from watching and learning on the salon floor is unique and very valuable to future employers. A hairdresser who has studied under an apprenticeship will already have developed customer service skills and a level of knowledge that may well surpass other training routes.

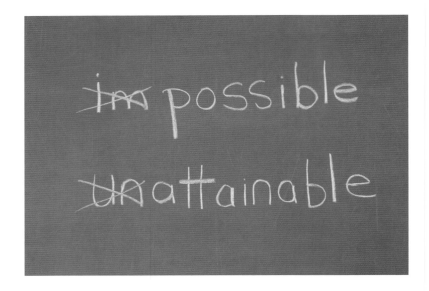

FULL-TIME STUDY AND QUALIFICATIONS

VRQ

The acronym stands for Vocational Related Qualification. This is a preparation-for-work qualification.

Many learners are unable to get an apprenticeship or may prefer to study at a further education college as a full-time learner. The type of qualification that can be undertaken in this way is a **VRQ**. This type of qualification can give the learner a large amount of knowledge and skills but they may require further learning or training once they begin working within the salon.

Whatever type of qualification or training someone has undertaken within the hair and beauty sector, it is imperative that a learner is prepared for a career where they will continue to keep training, developing and learning. Whether you train staff yourself, or employ someone who has qualified within another organisation, skills testing is a good way to ensure that you are happy with the person you are employing.

MORE ABOUT NVQS AND VRQS

As stated above, NVQ stands for National Vocational Qualification (in Scotland it is called an SVQ – Scottish Vocational Qualification). They are work-based qualifications that are achieved effectively by learning on the job. VRQ stands for Vocational Related Qualification and these qualifications are completed in a non-workplace environment. The level of each qualification represents the stage of progression the candidate is at. These range from levels 1–5 and indicate the following:
- Level 1 – junior
- Level 2 – basic young stylist / improver
- Level 3 – intermediate stylist
- Level 4 – competent stylist
- Level 5 – advanced stylist.

OTHER TYPES OF TRAINING

Manufacturers and suppliers run some great courses specialising in many areas such as hair up/bridal, men's cutting, advanced cutting techniques, and so on. It is advisable that all of the salon team regularly (at least once a year) attend some sort of course or seminar to keep themselves technically up to date. There are other educational options, too, as good manufacturers now run courses and seminars on reception skills, retail skills, etc. The cost of manufacturers' courses can vary, but some suppliers offer points you can redeem on training courses in relation to your spend on their products. It can be worth thinking about paying guest artists to visit your salons and do specialist one-to-one training in-house, although this will be expensive.

TRAINING TO BECOME A TECHNICIAN

For those who want to specialise in colour, the training will be exactly the same as for their cutting/styling counterparts, as NVQ Level 2 covers both elements. However, in some premium salons, hairdressers could specialise and gain a qualification at level 3 which covers the skills and knowledge needed to become a colour technician, or cutting and styling technician. The VRQ structure allows this type of qualification to be undertaken. It gives flexibility and allows further training and development to be recognised as part of a small but accredited qualification.

Further education for technicians

Suppliers and manufacturers such as L'Oréal, run some very good colour education programmes, including Colour Specialist Degrees. While these are expensive, these lengthy education programmes really do educate to a much higher level and enable you to charge premium prices for those who have successfully graduated through such a programme. There are shorter courses available too, which are also aimed at a senior level and cover areas such as specialist techniques and colour correction. There will also be new product and service innovations, so training on new products and launches can be done through their academies or in-house at your salons.

CITY & GUILDS

City & Guilds is steeped in history within the hairdressing industry and has been developing qualifications to support the industry for many years. It offers the traditional qualifications, such as the NVQ and VRQ, and has also developed a large number of short qualifications that lend themselves to the hairdressing or barbering industry. Many employees now want formal qualifications that are nationally, or even globally, recognised. By investing in staff development through **accredited** qualifications, you invest in the future of your business.

Training allows you to develop and expand your employees' skills in new areas of innovation, as well as up-skill staff in areas where they have not had experience or training in the past. This type of training and recognition of qualifications can also lead to expanding your business into other areas of the hairdressing or barbering industry, such as bridal hair, long hair work, etc.

Accredited
Officially authorised or recognised.

TRAINING AS A BEAUTY THERAPIST OR NAIL TECHNICIAN

Training to become a beauty therapist or nail technician can be undertaken in several ways. As with hairdressing, one training route is through an apprenticeship programme. However, in beauty therapy and nail service, this has historically not been the most popular avenue to pursue. The industry perception was that, unlike hairdressing, you could not learn on the job because of the issue of the private client/therapist relationship and the client's reluctance for a trainee to observe private treatments. However, apprenticeships are becoming more popular, and many spas and larger salons are now investing in apprentices to develop and train on the job.

FE (FURTHER EDUCATION) OR PRIVATE COLLEGE

By far the most popular way to train as a therapist or nail technician is through a further education college or a private college. These full-time courses train the therapist or nail technician to the standard of at least a level 3 qualification, which is the expected industry level. City & Guilds has been very involved with the beauty therapy and nail services industry, and their qualifications are highly regarded and recognised internationally. It is a real benefit for a therapist or nail technician who has trained to a level 3 standard and gained a City & Guilds qualification that these qualifications are recognised globally.

Different qualifications

There are several recognised qualifications, all of which require training at a college:

- CIBTAC (Confederation of International Beauty Therapy and Cosmetology)
- BABTC (British Association of Beauty Therapy and Cosmetology)
- IHBC (International Health & Beauty Council)
- CIDESCO (Comité International d'Esthétique et de Cosmétologie)
- CONFED (Confederation of Beauty Therapists)
- NVQ Level 2 and 3.

OTHER TYPES OF TRAINING

Many manufacturers also carry out training, with most of the main brands offering bespoke training procedures or protocols regarding how to use their products. Training that is product-based should always be heavily **subsidised**, if not complimentary, so ensure that you negotiate good terms for your team. Update-training and new product launches can be done in-house and should be offered regularly.

Subsidised
Part of the cost is paid for by another party.

CITY & GUILDS

City & Guilds has developed high quality qualifications for the beauty therapy industry for a long time. It has also developed a number of short qualifications that lend themselves to the beauty and nail industry. Many employers now want formal qualifications that are nationally, or even globally, recognised. Training allows you to develop and expand your employees' skills in new areas, as well as up-skill staff in areas where they have not had experience or training in the past. This type of training and recognition of qualifications can also lead to expansion of your business into other areas of the beauty and nail industry, such as stone therapy, permanent lashes, airbrush nails, electrical files, etc.

By investing in staff development through accredited qualifications, you invest in the future of your business.

TRAINING TO BECOME A MANICURIST/ NAIL TECHNICIAN

As with the beauty therapy industry, apprenticeships are uncommon for somebody who wants to train as a manicurist or nail technician. This means that training will be mainly conducted through colleges, although the course will be shorter and not necessarily as comprehensive as the training for beauty therapy.

FURTHER EDUCATION

As with hairdressing and beauty therapy, many manufacturers and suppliers run regular training programmes, which should be complimentary or subsidised. Training can also be conducted by suppliers in-salon, especially for updates and launches of new products and services.

LEARNING STYLES

Just as we are all different in the way we work and in our personalities, we all learn in different ways. The perfect team has a myriad of skills that deliver a great harmony and a good energy vibe that will be palpable to the customers. Identifying a team member's individual skills and developing them to optimise their talents is therefore a key role for the salon manager or owner. It requires analysis to find the right way for their team members to maximise their training and education and reach their full potential; self-assessment is a great way for team members to help you understand how they can best learn.

DIFFERENT LEARNING TYPES

There are many learning types:

- **action-orientated learners** like to be fully involved and learn through experience
- **reflective learners** learn through observing, analysing and reflecting on matters
- **theoretical learners** like to gather and review ideas, concepts and principals and learn by integrating these into a framework for action
- **practical learners** like to test out principles in practice and learn by trial and error.

Identifying how your team members learn will help you to come up with a bespoke programme of training and development that suits their individual personalities.

(Source: *The Successful Manager's Handbook* by Moi Ali (DK)

STAGES OF LEARNING

In order for training to be truly effective, the trainer has to understand the learning process. This involves four stages:
- **discovery** – the learning of new knowledge
- **incubation** – the practising of new knowledge
- **illumination** – the understanding of new knowledge
- **realisation** – becoming skilful and adept with the new knowledge.

It is said that we pick up information in a training environment in the following way:
- 10% of what we read
- 20% of what we hear
- 30% of what we see
- 50% of what we see and hear
- 70% of what is discussed.

You should use models, mood boards, products, colour and display materials to get your message across. Learning visually with coaching is always going to be the most productive way to get results; but it is calculated that a student will only retain 10% of the information from a training session. Understanding how our brains work is vital, too. Our thought processes move around four times faster than most people speak.

You should use a combination of all learning styles to get the best for individuals.

Our **logical left** side controls our analysing, reasoning, working out and mathematical elements. It is the exact, adult side of our minds. Whereas our **creative right** side governs our gut feelings, dreams, fantasies and artistic side. It can see similarities and is the playful, childlike side of our minds.

(Source: L'Oréal Professionnell)

THE LEARNING PROCESS

There are four stages of learning:
- **Stage 1**: Unconscious incompetence – we don't know that we don't know
- **Stage 2**: Conscious incompetence – we know that we don't know
- **Stage 3**: Conscious competence – we work at what we don't know
- **Stage 4**: Unconscious competence – we don't have to think about knowing it.

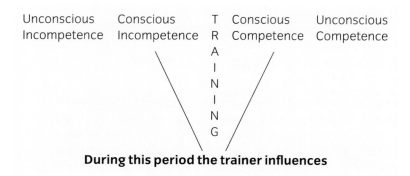

| Unconscious Incompetence | Conscious Incompetence | T R A I N I N G | Conscious Competence | Unconscious Competence |

During this period the trainer influences

For instance, a child rides his brother's bike. He is at stage 1 until he falls off then realises he can't do it. When he learns how to ride, he reaches stage 3 and thinks that he can do it and when he becomes an adult he reaches stage 4 where he does it without thinking. This is the way that you learn everything, so it is worth identifying which learning stage your team members are at and pointing out the learning process to them. When you next try to learn something new, ask yourself which stage in the learning process you are at.

The trainer can influence the employee during the 'conscious incompetence' and 'conscious competence' stages – it is far harder to influence in the other beginning or final stage because the employee will not be as open to learning at these stages, when they do things automatically.

THE KNOWLEDGE, ATTITUDE AND SKILL PYRAMID

Training is a foundation-building exercise of knowledge, attitude and skill.

Think of it in terms of this pyramid. Once the knowledge is established, the employee must want to go on to develop the skills to progress forward. The trainer cannot change attitudes, they can merely influence them.

ENCOURAGING PARTICIPATION

A good trainer is patient, understanding and empathetic and never undermines the student. They will exchange information, ideas, opinions and feelings and, above all, will invite participation, building relationships between themselves and their students.

The effective trainer develops a continual cycle that constantly evolves:

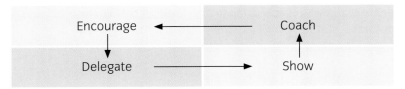

CREATING YOUR OWN TRAINING PROGRAMME

To really grow your own team, it is advisable to produce your own training programme of apprenticeship education, and higher education for team members who are already qualified. It might seem like a daunting task, but it is a great way to ensure that your junior team members turn into seniors who really do understand your company ethos.

If you are educating in-house, divide your training programme into three levels, and again into two areas: theory and practical. You may not be delivering the education yourself (for instance, product knowledge) as some elements will be done through a supplier; but you can create a checklist of each level and what you want the trainees to cover before they move onto the next stage. This will help them to understand where they are in their training programme and what they need to cover to move on. It is a great way to track their progress via reviews and assessments, with input from those tutoring them in both theory and practical sessions.

THEORY AND OTHER ELEMENTS

Do not forget that in theory education you should also be covering aspects such as consultation skills, effective communication, role play and other service-related topics, not just technical and product theory.

Many of the college education programmes will not teach the customer service and business elements of being a great therapist, nail technician, hairdresser or colourist, so you will have to ensure that employees are trained in these areas. It is useful to devise your own programme of education to develop your team to their full potential, and start talking to them right from the start about what you will be monitoring and, therefore, will expect from them later.

REVIEWING A TEAM MEMBER'S EDUCATIONAL NEEDS

During the development process, training and education will form part of the natural progression of your team members. It is a good idea to carry out a self-assessment for your team members so they are discovering for themselves which skills they feel they need to develop and how they think they are progressing. Encouraging reflection on their performance and their education programme is healthy and enables the employee to play an active role in their ongoing development.

As managers, you need to create a personal development plan for all of your team members, which can be jointly agreed between you and your employees. Sometimes practice and experience alone will improve the skills that need development; on other occasions, bespoke training will need to be delivered (either within or outside the salon environment) to achieve the objectives. Set time frames by which skills need to be developed and honed, and clarify how you are going to get there together. Use this check list to help you:

- **define** the need for the training and the outcome you wish to achieve
- **plan** the best time for the development activity and training
- **describe** how the training will happen – when, how, with whom, and the cost
- **record** the results and outcome, once training is completed.

TRAINING AGREEMENT

It is useful to create a training agreement with your team members that states that if they leave before a certain period of time, a proportional cost of the training is paid back to the company. After all, the skill is one that will benefit them in the future, so it is not unreasonable to expect them to pay back some of your investment in them. Remember to confirm the cost and ensure they are aware of the agreement and the policy before the training starts, giving them a signed copy and keeping one for your files.

RESISTANCE TO CHANGE

Constant growing and evolving means change – not only for the team member, but also for their colleagues. People can be afraid of change and development, as we are all creatures of habit and dislike being out of our comfort zones; so it is understandable that teams may resist change.

Young, inexperienced students often learn new information more quickly than older, more experienced students. Once fully trained at unconscious competence level, some senior team members may resist training. But if we can encourage them to undertake training and development, it may give them a fresh perspective and a new lease of life. Getting past the 'mental lock' and challenging them to embrace new skills is vital. In order for them to get out of their comfort zone, plenty of praise and encouragement is needed. The 'mental lock' could be a confidence issue, or the harbouring of a negative attitude towards becoming a 'student' again. Watching someone perform a task looks easy when they are at 'unconscious competence' stage, and when the student tries to perform the same task they may lose confidence if they fail. This encourages a negative attitude to the task and the training.

MAKING CHANGES

It is essential to win support for any changes you make, whether it is educating yourself, finding a new manufacturer, moving premises, bringing in a new team member or merely changing your working practices. It is important to find the key influencers among team members and get them on side by fully explaining the reason for the change. Most people will be positive if you point out the reasons and benefits and clearly identify how they personally will benefit from the change. Ideally, it is good to involve key team members in the decision-making process before the change comes about, so they feel empowered to help the change work and explain the benefits to the team.

CHANGING HABITS

Habits are hard to break; it has been estimated that 21 days is needed to break a habit – but it can be done.

Try this fun exercise with your team to demonstrate that habits are hard to break:

Clasp your hands together, putting one thumb over the other. Now reverse the habit. One way will be more comfortable to you and it has nothing to do with left or right handedness.

SUMMARY

It is vital to understand the routes to qualifications in our sector: both as essential interview and recruitment benchmarks and to develop and evolve the team members for whom we are responsible. Create a training plan that is regularly evaluated and reviewed at appraisals.

Understanding how we learn is vital to becoming a competent educator, so it is just as important to educate the trainers, too. Even if you decide not to develop your own training programme, make sure you have a plan of education for all levels of your team, and ensure you are constantly updating your staff members' skills, thereby offering an excellent technical standard to customers. Remember to include service skills as part of your ongoing programme.

See training and education for what it really is: a tailored way for you to refine skills and maximise abilities so that the salon and the individual can benefit financially. Scrimping on training and education will lead to a demotivated, stale team. They need to know that you are investing in their future.

CHAPTER 4
CUSTOMER SERVICE

This chapter looks at one of most important elements for achieving success – defining and delivering consistently good service. We will explore some analogies and principles you can adopt to ensure your team are focused on client care. We will also look at the procedures they need to follow to make sure the customer experience is the best it can be, including positive nonverbal communication and body language. It will cover retailing skills and how to create the perfect retail environment. It also looks at how to deal with things when they go wrong, which they will from time to time, and how to exercise damage limitation from the start.

CUSTOMERS WHO DO NOT RETURN

Statistics suggest that 60% of salon customers do not come back.

That is quite a shocking statistic to start a chapter with! But further analysis can tell us why some customers leave and never return:

- 1% die
- 3% move away
- 5% buy from a friend
- 9% prefer a competitor
- 14% are dissatisfied with the product
- 68% perceive an attitude of indifference in the service they receive.

(Source: L'Oréal Professionnel)

This statistic clearly demonstrates why good customer service is something all salons should have in common. It is clearly why our clients vote with their feet. The facts speak for themselves – get it wrong and we will all lose out, whatever our salon type, price or brand ethos.

WHAT IS CUSTOMER SERVICE?

Customer service is a way of thinking – not a department.

In an increasingly impersonal and 'virtual' world, the hair or beauty salon is becoming unique in its old-fashioned core-service values. As hairdressers, therapists or nail technicians, you enjoy a special client-facing relationship that simply is not replicated on such a regular basis in any other industry – where people know their customer's name and enjoy such a uniquely personal relationship. Its importance is therefore growing in significance and is a strength we should value, verbalise, encourage, educate and strengthen among our teams.

DELIVERING CONSISTENCY

By far the hardest part of maintaining our standards is delivering consistency. It simply is not good enough to give a 'one out of ten' service for one visit and a 'nine out of ten' service for the next. In order to become known for something, we have to be delivering regularly – and having a reputation for great client care is no exception. Word-of-mouth recommendation is by far the greatest asset you have for encouraging new business, and people only recommend you if they experience a high level of consistency.

In other industries, that are not reliant on people, consistency can be easier to ensure but in ours it is a challenge. Think of a sandwich bar, where the owner has to ensure that the prawn salad sandwich is as good on Wednesday as it was on Monday. It is not hard to write a manual to describe in detail how to make the sandwich – how many dollops of mayonnaise, etc. It may not even matter if the person serving the sandwich is different – the customer might not even notice.

In the hairdressing and beauty industry, you are reliant on people to deliver the service – so how do you go about standardising people? People have feelings; they have good days and they have 'off' days – they are governed by their emotions. It is not as simple as developing a formula and sticking to it. And even if people didn't experience all those service-affecting challenges the treatment you deliver to your customers is ever-changing because your customers' needs are constantly evolving. People's hair and beauty needs develop and change between appointments so their service and treatment experience is going to be different every time. It is, therefore, a tangible challenge to aim for consistent service. To meet it, you have to realise that delivering this consistency must be the aim for your teams – above and beyond anything else.

CUSTOMER SERVICE

Looking after your customers and making them feel special, comfortable, welcomed and valued is a skill that you need to demonstrate and teach to your team, leading by example all the way. The successful salon manager is one who really understands how to deliver a great customer experience and demonstrates this to their team, acting as a service role model. It is not an easy thing to teach and educate. It is far easier to train someone how to cut a geometric bob, or perform a great manicure, than it is to show them how to make people feel like they want to come back.

MAKING PEOPLE FEEL SPECIAL

This is a key element in the success of a salon, and trying to filter down a client care ethos is a challenge for everyone in the industry. There will be team members who are natural service givers – smiley, happy people who instinctively have a talent for making people feel good. If you see this skill in any of your team, at whatever level, recognise it and cultivate it. It may be that a new trainee is getting fantastic feedback from your customers; if so, you would be wise to see how you could nurture that talent and filter it through to other team members – for instance, making the trainee the 'buddy' during induction periods.

Good service can be hard to define. People generally know a good customer service experience from a bad one, but sometimes find it difficult to pinpoint what makes it such. It might be the subtle use of a name, the nod of recognition, the smile of acknowledgment when the receptionist is on the phone and busy, the remembrance of a seemingly insignificant detail that makes the client feel valued, the knowing when to intervene in a situation, the judging of when to chat and when to leave a customer in peace. There are a number of nuances that make up a great customer experience, and it is our job to instill these in our team members so they are encouraged to develop a service-giving instinct.

One thing is definite: if it is difficult to define, it is difficult to educate and teach and therefore we cannot ensure good service by simply trying to write a rule book for our teams to follow – if only it were that simple!

WHAT MAKES GREAT SERVICE?

Service is personal and 'in the eye of the beholder' so you may disagree with my definition of great client care. But I think it should include the following elements:

- warm, welcoming, natural and 'real'
- good eye contact
- use of name before prompt (after all, we know it!)
- good interpretation of body language
- intuitive to client's wishes
- pre-empting of client's needs
- matching the customer's pace and speed to show empathy for their feelings/time limitations
- finding out the individual's needs and working to meet them
- the personal touch – the indefinable 'X factor' that makes people feel special and want to come back – normally demonstrated by the service giver showing a genuine interest in the customer
- sensitivity to situations
- going over and above what is required – surpassing expectations
- checking to see that everything is OK
- acting on what has been reported back
- anticipating client's reactions.

CULTURAL EXPECTATIONS

The British service sensibility is far and away different from that of our American cousins. The 'How are you' question (that is not really a question) and the 'Have a nice day' throwaway line do not really fit with the British perception of service. We have a more grounded, sincere list of requirements to meet. We do not tend to like the scripted, contrived material that is recited without feeling or sentiment. Do not be tempted to develop these Americanisms thinking that, if you do not, you are not giving good service.

It is better to really understand what your customer wants and train your team to get in tune with finding out for themselves, than be tempted to go with a 'one size fits all' approach to your customer care. Have the courage to throw away the script and have a company policy on customer service which simply states 'Meet and exceed the customers' needs – whatever they are'. With guidance, training and education, you can empower your team to deliver it in a way that suits their individual personalities.

Creating a customer service culture in our workplaces is not easy, but doing so has palpable benefits.

THE CLIENT'S WISH LIST

Good customer care cannot be contrived or scripted. It is not about trotting out a company policy when you answer the phone or getting your teams to deliver a word-perfect greeting. This is not good service.

Good customer service cannot really be manufactured. It has to be innate – something that comes naturally from the individual. It is a sensibility – a skill we can develop, if we work hard. It really cannot be perceived to be 'good service' if it is too standardised. The whole point of service is about finding the 'wish list' of the client, then ticking it off. Answering the phone within a target time is great, but it is far better to answer it sincerely after letting it ring a little longer, than to recite a standard greeting without sincerity.

OLYMPIC TORCH ANALOGY

A useful analogy to consider can be that of the Olympic torch. For the time that each customer is in the care of your team members, try to get them to envisage that, for that moment, they are in charge of holding the Olympic torch (the client). Asking them to visualise passing the client like a baton in a relay race is a great way for them to think about their service responsibilities while the client is in their care. When they hand over the client to the next operator, they are technically handing over control of keeping the Olympic flame alive while the client is with the next team member.

This Olympic torch analogy really helps to symbolise how important giving good customer care is and how the responsibility for looking after all the client's needs falls to the team member concerned while the client is in their care. It becomes the responsibility of the team member to take control of those needs, whatever they are and whatever they concern, during their period of ownership. Verbally passing the client over by introducing them to the next operator (eg from receptionist to stylist, from junior to technician) is an indication that the client's wants and needs are now under the ownership of the next team member.

USER EXPERIENCE (UXP)

The term user experience (UXP) was first introduced in Book 1 Chapter 9. You should by now be familiar with imagining that your customer's experience with you is a journey which they take. Training and educating your teams on what you want the journey to consist of and how you want them to deliver it is therefore essential, and personal to your salon and its ethos. It is key to ensure that the customer journey is constantly monitored and evaluated, so you can instantly see where gaps in the service are appearing and sort any cracks out before they spread.

CUSTOMER JOURNEY

You may be getting parts of the journey absolutely right, but other areas may be weaker. Find out where you are falling down by sending in a mystery shopper to let you know. Make sure your team visualise, with you, the customer's journey through the salon, so they can ensure they are doing everything they can during their service to make it as smooth and slick as possible. You can try mapping this into stages to help make sure the right team members are responsible for the different parts of the journey.

Stage 1 – arrival at reception
The client will check in and be greeted by a receptionist. Then she may walk through a retail area to leave her coat/collect a gown, etc, before being escorted to the waiting area.

Stage 2 – waiting area
Make sure someone is responsible for regularly checking this area so that clients are not kept waiting too long. The operator should meet and greet their client from here, if they have not done so already. If they are not busy it is advisable to ask them to wait and greet clients – especially new ones – at reception.

Stage 3 – the service itself
In hairdressing this might involve the backwash, but it will always firstly involve the consultation, involving the stylist, technician and apprentice. In beauty, the therapist will take the client straight through for treatment following the consultation procedure, which should include preparing them for how much clothing to remove, and how to position themselves on the couch.

The operator should describe what will happen during the treatment in detail so the client knows exactly what to expect.

Stage 4 – the home care regime/retail advice

The client may be escorted by the operator back to reception to pay, and her care is temporarily handed back to the receptionist.

Stage 5 – the close

The client is given the recommended timings of the follow-up treatment plan by her operator and hopefully re-books her next appointment before leaving.

Good communication at every stage is essential to a smooth and enjoyable client journey. Remember, we cannot over-communicate. In order for clients to feel truly at home, we need to ensure they know where they are, what facilities are around them, who is looking after them and the duration of the stage. For example, in the waiting area – it is not enough just to ask a client to take a seat. You should explain where to sit, where the toilets are, how to get refreshments, how long they are going to be there and who is coming to get them (and when) in order for them to feel totally comfortable.

AIDA PRINCIPLE

In marketing, the well-known AIDA principle is deemed to form the basis of all our retailing, advertising and selling. Its ideals are said to mirror consumer behaviour:

- **A**ttention
- **I**nterest
- **D**esire
- **A**ction.

Its philosophy is that we engage our customer through these steps. You start by getting attention, and then you create interest. Next you build desire and finally you stimulate action.

It is worth taking note of the AIDA principle, making sure your marketing is designed to stimulate the required actions and that your team are aware of these consumer behavioural patterns. Its relevance to our industry, I believe, is that it helps cement the maxim that it is our job to draw to our client's **attention** the services and treatments available, and not assume that every customer has encyclopaedic knowledge of our price list's contents! The effective operator will make sure the client is fully aware of potential services that may be of **interest** and gauge their **desire** to achieve the result and hence **action** the plan.

Make sure your team members not only think about the stages they are directly involved in, but are constantly looking out for any salon client at any stage of their journey who may need assistance, to help cultivate a service ethos among the team.

THE PERFECT CONSULTATION

Developing an excellent 'chair-side (or couch-side) manner' is key. The bulk of my in-house training and education is spent on teaching my team how to conduct the perfect consultation, because if they learn how to consult well, and properly, I know that customer satisfaction levels will increase. Perfecting the art of expert consulting will ensure that team members know how to work out what their customers want, and if they know that, they are more than likely to be able to deliver then exceed that expectation, creating a desire for repeat visits.

Developing an excellent 'chair- or couch-side' manner is crucial to building a loyal and trusting clientele.

STAGES OF A GREAT CONSULTATION

A great consultation should discover and embrace the following stages.

Visit expectation

What are your clients expecting the treatment/service to deliver today? For instance, if the client has very dark brown hair and is hoping to be a perfect extra light blonde, are they assuming that you will be able to deliver that on today's visit, when it might be a long-term treatment plan? Make sure the expectation is discussed and an agreed timing of treatments is established.

In-depth analysis

The operative might be a therapist, technician, or stylist, but they must always conduct an analysis of the client's skin, hair, nails or scalp. For therapists, I would insist they fill in a consultation form in order to form a proper technical diagnosis and ascertain any treatment contraindications. Looking at a client's style of dress, their jewellery and accessories, etc, can help us make judgements and ascertain if their style is classic, contemporary, adventurous or understated. It helps to do this before the gowning procedure. Any operator, regardless of what service they are performing, should carry out an assessment, looking at the relevant areas/factors:

- skin tone
- cool/warm and contrast/blend analysis (use colour fans to ascertain)
- colour profile (does the client want to whisper, shout or scream her colour result)
- skin type
- eye colour
- natural colour/percentage grey/white
- hair texture
- hair density
- scalp health
- hair health and condition
- skin condition
- nail condition
- factors which may influence the treatment/service
- contraindications (pregnancy, etc).

Physical communication

This is an important part of trust-building between client and operator. For instance, in hairdressing, putting hands on a client's shoulder during a consultation will break down barriers and help the client feel more relaxed so the operator can look at their hair and scalp thoroughly.

Concerns

Any specific concerns in the areas above should be discussed in more detail.

Lifestyle

A client's lifestyle will affect their choice of service – this includes not only the amount of time they can devote to their grooming, but matters that may affect it, like swimming every day or night shift working. This is essential information that operators need to find out.

Maintenance

A home-care regime and maintenance programme is an important part of the service offered to clients. It is vital to give customers a service or treatment that they can look after and there may be additional advice to give them or tools to recommend in order for them to do so.

Short-term issues

A client may have holidays coming up, potential sun exposure, etc, which all have to be taken into account to ensure the correct advice is given. Unless we ask open questions, important information like this (that the client may not realise is relevant) may get missed.

Long-term treatment plan

It is essential to work towards an agreed goal or work out a programme of maintenance and ongoing service and treatment in order to make sure you really understand your client's needs.

COLOUR CONSULTATIONS

In hairdressing, the colour consultation is perhaps the most important to get right. Training your team to work out whether a client is warm or cool, and whether they are a contraster (and clear, strong colours suit them) or a blend (and muted colours suit them) is a skill that you can market pricewise.

It also helps to deliver a better result, technically, as does L'Oréal's 'whisper, shout or scream' analogy to the final colour result. A 'whisper' is a client who does not want her colour result to show (classic and understated), a 'shout' client wants her colour to look more obvious (contemporary, perhaps), and a 'scream' client is willing to go very bold and try anything colourwise (adventurous). Discovering these key elements will really help to deliver a great technical result.

THE LONG-TERM TREATMENT PLAN

Every client can be considered a 'work in progress' and, as such, we need to define a long-term programme of treatment, not only to retain our clients, but also to ensure we are delivering the full service package. With industry research confirming that client visit frequency levels are dropping across UK salons, we know that the average client is spending more per visit and having more services conducted but is coming in less frequently. Therefore, encouraging repeat booking is a key element to retaining our clientele's visit rates and improving them.

The most natural way to encourage our customers to visit more frequently is through creating a long-term treatment plan. Think of it like making sure they always leave with a reason to return, rather than just reciting the usual line, 'Would you like to book your next appointment before you leave today?' A good operator will be lining up a programme of treatment over the coming months to optimise results and satisfy the long-term treatment goal.

HOW TO RETAIL

Retail sales should be a natural progression as the result of a detailed and thorough consultation. Retail experts tell us that knowledge (ours) equals trust (from our customers), and that great salespeople have certain qualities in common: they listen more than they talk, are honest, do not knock the competition, smile, back up their promises and always talk about benefits rather than features to personalise the sale.

RETAIL ADVICE

However, it is worth encouraging a 'don't sell – just advise' mentality among your teams. Adopting this maxim will make them feel more relaxed about giving a good diagnosis and will encourage the correct attitude to retailing – it should always be viewed as an extension of the professional service and *never* a hard sell. We must make sure we always view our retail in the right way, too. It is unnerving to tell people they have to sell something. But tell them that it is their job to offer the right advice and the sales should come naturally as and when they are necessary.

How to do it

A total lack of retail sales would concern me – and not just because it is an income stream that has not been maximised. More significantly, it signals that the customer has not received the full UXP that they should have done and the salon has underdelivered. Great advice and recommendation usually means that a client wants to buy into a home-care regime to carry on the service at home, so it is not uncommon to find that failure to retail signifies a failure to recommend adequately and that a substandard consultation is the root of the problem.

Retail advice should not be a last minute, eg the 'Are you all right for shampoo?' or, 'Did you need any cleanser?' style of conversation at the close of the client visit. Questions like this just demonstrate that the operator has not done their job properly. Good home-care advice should be the result of a detailed analysis before the treatment starts, with the correct products being used throughout and a natural sell-through of the items needed to create the prescribed home-care package as a conclusion.

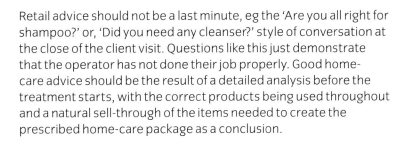

NONVERBAL COMMUNICATION

We communicate visually and nonverbally all the time through our:

- eye contact
- body language
- gestures and facial expressions
- clothes and accessories.

Positive body language and behaviour is vital and a skill worth training your team to deliver. Body language makes up 55% of what we communicate to another person. The way an operator stands, makes eye contact and uses facial expressions will all give a message to their client about them, their attitude and their emotions.

Positive examples

Positive examples of nonverbal communication might include:

- an individual tilting their head to one side indicates that they are interested in what someone is saying
- a client with her legs crossed towards them means she is comfortable with them.

Negative examples

Negative examples might be:

- someone crossing their arms can make them appear defensive
- standing with their hands on their hips is a sign of aggression.

Picking up signals

Teach your operators to mirror the customer's positive body language for maximum impact. You need to train your team to pick up the positive buying signals they find from reading body language properly. Remember:

- eye contact should be direct to show interest (not looking someone in the eye is possibly the worst body language of all as it indicates disinterest)
- voice tones should be matching, seating position should be matching
- leaning forward shows attentiveness, tense posture indicates withdrawal
- clasped hands suggest eagerness, but folded hands indicate defensiveness
- feet facing forward shows attentiveness, but legs crossed form a barrier (especially if a foot is pointing away from the speaker).

THE ART OF LISTENING

Listening is a skill that needs practice. A good listener must control their ego (and demonstrate that they are only interested in the other person), their intellect (not using technical jargon or blinding the client with science) and emotions (never arguing or losing control) if they are going to be effective. Hearing is not the same as listening; listening only comes when we understand what others are saying.

To listen well we need to give our complete attention and show a genuine interest in what the client is saying. We must not interrupt or put words into others' mouths. Above all, we must develop an open mind so we can pick up on any clues and stop ourselves from making preconceived judgements.

'SMILEABILITY'

Your smile is what people see first. We all think we smile much of the time, but only one third of people have naturally open and smiling faces, while one third have neutral faces (which can go readily from a smile to a serious, intense look) and one third of people have serious faces, whether they think they are smiling or not. If you are in the smiling third you have an advantage – people perceive you as open and friendly; they will be more receptive to your ideas and you can also convey bad news more easily. If you are in the final, serious third, you may be smiling on the inside but your face reflects doom and gloom on the outside and this is what you communicate. Perception is reality in the eyes of the beholder.

EYE CONTACT

The eyes are the only part of your central nervous system that directly connects with another person, so good eye communication means more than just a fleeting glance. To look sincerely and steadily at another person takes between 5 and 15 seconds. Making this a habit is vital for your teams, so they when they are under pressure they can maintain a confident eye contact without seemingly needing to think about it.

Three i's of eye contact
These are:

- intimacy   – 10 seconds to 1 minute
- intimidation   – 10 seconds to 1 minute
- involvement   – our day-to-day use

One-to-one communication is naturally 5–10 seconds before looking away, so this is the ideal to strive for; but be aware of the fact that most people under pressure have a desire to look anywhere other than at the listener. This nervousness undermines credibility. Also, beware of the slow blink – keeping your eyelids closed for 2–3 seconds – as it conveys the message that you do not want to be there!

Analyse your next conversation – work out where you generally look – you do not look in both eyes; either left or right, but it is impossible to look in both. In one-to-one conversations the eyes tend to move around a face. If you feel uncomfortable try looking at a person's forehead – just above the eyes. Remember, however, that you will not feel as 'in touch' with them.

Staying at someone's eye level or lower during the consultation process is key as this makes the client automatically feel more comfortable and at ease with the operator.

You may think your customers will not pick up on these subtle signs without knowing the above, but instinctively people can read another person's body language – so address these signs with your team.

It is worth educating your team to step into the customer's shoes to develop a real empathy with them. Staff should learn to encourage interest nonverbally by nodding, then reflecting on the problem by using key words and summarising back to the client the concerns raised, to check that agreement has been reached on the course of action. Listening really well will help establish the hook. Train operators to use visual aids and leaflets to help reinforce information, and use their link-selling skills to highlight products that complement each other and which will deliver the required results.

CREATING A RETAIL ENVIRONMENT

I find the greatest retail success comes from a professional, diagnostic environment. Creating an advice area or accompanying it with tools to correctly assess gives weight to the prescribed products and recommendations. A good consultation cannot be done standing behind a chair. It needs to be done on a one-to-one basis, with eye levels matching, and both operator and client informally seated, ideally side by side, so that the discussion engages the client and feels professional but without creating unnecessary barriers.

SHOW AND TELL

It is advisable to make sure your operators think about and do the following.
- confirm their consultation diagnosis and, when selecting products to use in the salon, explain why they are using them
- show and demonstrate the features and benefits of the product while the treatment or service is being conducted, explaining how to use it

- position the product in front of the client after use for them to see it, pick it up, touch it, smell it, feel it and examine it; merely placing the product in front of them is not enough

- explain the benefit after the product has been used and demonstrate it to them visually, ie show hair feeling less static, etc
- follow up at reception by showing them the product again in a 'this is what we used for your dry scalp today' manner
- learn to leave it at that; if the client does not want to purchase it, that is their prerogative, the operator's job is done.

THE PROFESSIONAL RECOMMENDATION

Try to educate your team on retailing by likening it to a trip to the dentist – although a little more exciting! The hygienist would not be afraid to tell you why you need to floss your teeth every day, show you how to do it, then place the floss in your hands so you can get familiar with it. They would also not let you leave without educating you about what you need to do at home to get the same result.

It is wise to point out that sometimes the counter objections (that it is too expensive, for instance) may be coming from them and not the customer! If their perception is that their mother would not pay that much money for a moisturiser, they may be subconsciously passing on these internal negative attitudes by assuming their client would not either.

There are now some innovative machines for diagnosing skin, scalp and hair. These provide a great visual opportunity to analyse and prescribe the right products, as well as making your assessments feel more scientific and demonstrating more clearly the need for good retail products to address concerns.

THE RETAIL ENVIRONMENT

Follow my top tips to help create the right retail environment.

Hair workstation

This requires good product placement, a nearby retail area to select product from, minimal information on sections (leaflets, flyers) but access to it.

Treatment room

You need tester bars located nearby so clients can sample and try products, diagnosis forms on which to prescribe from stocked ranges, as well as other retail opportunities such as self-tan.

Technical area

Colour glazes and glosses are a great retail opportunity to minimise fade and refresh colour between visits, as well as colour lock professional home-care products. So ensure there is easy access to nearby retail and inform clients by marketing and promoting specific technical products.

Manicure area

Nail polishes are often purchased to top up colour at home between visits, so ensure the colour bar of polishes is nearby to attract interest in other colours too.

NEVER UNDERDELIVER TO REPEAT CUSTOMERS!

It is very easy to fall into the trap of underdelivering to regular or repeat customers and not giving them the service and attention they deserve. 'Mrs Jones won't mind waiting' or 'Miss Brown won't need her scalp analysed, she's a regular' can be fatal assumptions on our part. It is important to realise that regular customers will go elsewhere if they are taken for granted, and a new salon will offer them the full 'bells and whistles' service (until they, too, make the fatal mistake of not suggesting anything new, not listening and assuming their needs have not changed).

Remind your team that they never get a second chance to make a first impression!

PROCEDURES TO FOLLOW

There are several potential legalities that you need to bear in mind when considering your customer service and UXP. It is prudent, while the industry is still unregulated, to ensure we do all we can to protect our salons.

SKIN TESTING

Although there is no legislation as such regarding skin testing, industry benchmarks have been set following recommendations from manufacturers.

Always follow the manufacturer's instructions on skin testing

Every client should follow your salon's skin allergy test procedure. Clients who have not had a colour application in your salon within the preceding three months should undergo a patch test, ideally using the product that is going to be used or, if undecided, the product range by the manufacturer, 48 hours before any colour procedure. If there is no sensitivity or reaction, the procedure can be carried out. Once the client has become a regular salon client, subsequent periodic retesting is advised, at least annually; so make sure clients know they may have to undergo the skin allergy test procedure before starting further technical services.

Reactions can appear suddenly after years of safely using the same product, so train your operators to log and record conducting skin tests. Do not go without testing for longer than three months – even if the client is a regular salon client; if the product has not been applied within the preceding three months, you may find yourself negligent.

To carry out a skin test, simply mix some neat product with water (not peroxide) and dab a patch behind the ear. Tell the client to leave the product there for 48 hours without washing it away and look for any signs of reaction.

New or transient clients who want colour services should not be seen without a patch test being conducted. Some clients insist they happily use the exact product at another salon, but failure to carry out the procedure could leave you liable.

DISCLAIMERS

As a salon owner or manager you need to protect yourself against
any possible liabilities. As we have considered in Book 1, Chapter 5,
it is prudent to ensure you are covered regarding insurance for any
incidence of damage to clothes and personal belongings. Make sure
you clearly display signs such as 'X salon does not accept any liability
for any loss or damage to any personal belongings. We advise all
clients to adhere to our strict gowning procedure and failure to do
so may result in possible damage to clothing during some technical
processes, which is entirely at the owner's risk'.

However, there may be times when treatments and services are
conducted against your professional judgement. Of course, this
should never happen, but from time to time it may be necessary
to ask a client to sign a disclaimer which helps diminish your
responsibility legally should the treatment encounter problems.
We do not work in a theoretical salon environment, we work in a
real one, and from time to time it may help to protect you if you
complete a form which helps absolve responsibility.

For example, a client may demand that you colour her eyebrows
using a matching colour formula from her hair to get a more natural
result. It may be that you refuse, but that she wishes to use the
product (extreme example, I know, but there are many cases I can
think of!). You could not allow the client to use the product without
signing a disclaimer; but if you refuse, she may think you are being
petty and you may lose her. Liability forms have their place, but in
general, if you need to sign one for any reason, you really should not
be doing the service or treatment in the first place, so bear that in
mind. They do have a certain amount of legal weight, but ultimately
if you go against your professional opinion, they are difficult to
uphold. However, once a client has signed a disclaimer, it does limit
the chances of any action being taken on their part.

DEALING WITH CUSTOMER COMPLAINTS

We are not going to get it right all of the time; in fact, the law of averages dictates that we are going to get it wrong sometimes, if not quite often. It would be foolish to think otherwise. In fact, it is suggested that for every client who voices a complaint, 10 other customers feel the same way but have not bothered to tell you and have just voted with their feet – scary statistics.

However, every customer complaint can be seen as a learning experience and a well-handled complaint is an opportunity to strengthen customer relationships. Normally, if your standards are high, the root of the customer problem lies somewhere in a poor consultation. If you have not correctly assessed a customer's needs, what hope is there of meeting them, let alone surpassing expectations? So I often find that a consultation that is not detailed enough, with no boundaries and benchmarks set, or where visual aids have not been used to clarify the service or treatment that is going to be conducted, can lead to a lack of understanding about the end result.

COMPLAINT PROCEDURES

If a customer does feel the need to complain, there are certain procedures to follow. It is worth running through them with all of your team members, so they know how to deal with a problem before it gets to you!

What to do

Make sure to carry out the following actions.

- Take the client away to a quiet space away from reception where other clients cannot hear – go to a more private area with seating and give the client your full focus, without any distractions.
- Sit down at eye level and allow the customer to speak, without interruption. Do not be tempted to jump in and correct facts, let them 'get it off their chest' and let off steam first, before putting your side.
- Nod in silent agreement while they are speaking, to let them know that you are listening and understanding their frustrations. You are not agreeing, you are empathising.
- Once they have completely finished, and without admitting any liability, tell them that you understand how they are feeling and that you are going to deal with it for them and sort it out.

- Offer them a drink or refreshment, and ask them what outcome they are looking for (this really helps you figure out how you can sort the problem). For instance, it may become apparent on rare occasions, that a client is 'acting up' and merely looking for a refund or not to pay. If they are not willing for you to make them happy, this may become apparent.
- Tell them that you want to resolve their complaint – it may be wise to have a policy of 'redo' instead of refund. If you refund their bill there and then, there is no chance you can restore their goodwill and turn the situation around. Some of your best customers can be those that were previous complaints, so work at making them happy instead of sending them to another salon where your brand name and reputation could be damaged.
- Go off and investigate the matter, then come back and state, very gently, what the situation is from your side. It is wise not to admit liability, but assure them that you very much want to make them feel happy.
- Agree a plan of action that the client feels happy with, and then implement the plan. Make sure you track and monitor each return visit and get involved in all future consultations.
- However many revisits it takes to get it right, make sure all are complimentary until the client is entirely satisfied with the service that they originally paid for.

'I'LL SORT THAT OUT FOR YOU ...'

Just saying 'I'll sort that out for you…' is a guaranteed way to upset your customers. You are not sorting it out for them; you are sorting it out for you and your salon! If someone has cause to complain, there is an issue and, as the salon manager or owner, it is your problem, so do not make them feel that, in dealing with it, you are doing them the favour. They are doing you the favour for bringing it to your attention.

WHEN TO WALK AWAY...

The important thing is that the complaint is resolved satisfactorily on both sides, but not all clients have the best intentions when telling us about a poor experience. Some people are simply going to 'try it on' and test your patience, or look to find fault to avoid full payment.

Warning bells

I tend to hear warning bells ring when a client:

- has trouble committing to a 'wish list' during the consultation stage (I train my team to get their supervisor if they cannot visually confirm the boundaries)
- refuses to be specific about their requirements
- embellishes team behaviour and other staff can attest to their difficulty
- is rude, aggressive or behaving in an unacceptable manner.

If any of these instances occur, politely suggest that your salon is not capable of meeting the customer's requirements and suggest that they may be happier seeking an alternative.

SUMMARY

The hardest factor to put our finger on, the most difficult to educate and develop, yet the most crucial element of our salons' success, is delivering great and consistent service. Can service be taught? It does tend to be innate, yet we can train our teams to recognise great customer care and try and cultivate it for themselves. Getting it right is critical; but getting it wrong is all too common. Try to find naturally good service givers among your team and get them to mentor younger team members. This can encourage them to develop the skill of finding out what makes people 'tick' and learn the value of how that can translate into a great business.

Envisage and share your vision of the client's visit journey, then give your teams the training they need to deliver it – encouraging them to develop the perfect 'chair-side manner'. If your practical and technical work as a salon is up to speed, there will be no such thing as a bad haircut or facial, just a poor consultation; so ongoing education and development of consulting skills will be a vital element to success.

However, it is just as important to educate our teams on how to handle things when they go wrong, because this will happen from time to time. Even if the team member themselves is not ultimately responsible for dealing with the complaint, it is wise to regularly update and educate the team on how to handle complaints and the procedures to follow.

CHAPTER 5
DISCIPLINARY PROCEDURE

This chapter covers the essential knowledge you need for a basic understanding of your responsibilities regarding employment law. We will look at the basics of disciplinary procedure so you can handle situations when things go wrong with your team, and how to carry out a disciplinary procedure, as well as creating your own grievance policy within the salon. Employment law is a specialist matter and cannot possibly be covered in depth in this chapter, but I will give you an overview of your responsibilities.

EMPLOYER'S RESPONSIBILITIES

As an employer, one of your main duties is to be fair to your employees. From time to time, it will be necessary to discipline staff and to do this you need to make sure you are compliant and acting within the law. Failure to do so will be costly, both financially and to your reputation. It is important to be recognised as being a fair employer, so getting it wrong is not an option.

Disciplinary procedure is not about sacking people – but involves pointing out issues and, hopefully, correcting behaviour. Ideally, you want every employee to carry out the services and treatments you sell in the right manner. This will not always happen, so you need to follow a process to deal with any problems and use your structure and review procedures to flag up any concerns before they become major issues.

EMPLOYEE EXPECTATIONS

First, you need to be certain that your employees are fully aware of what is expected from them. You must communicate this through:
- induction manuals
- job descriptions
- appraisals
- company rules and regulations
- supervisory or managerial feedback
- regular communication through staff meetings.

QUESTIONS TO ASK

You cannot discipline people for what they are doing wrong if they do not know what they have to do in the first place. You can never assume that some elements of their performance are a given; you need to cover all the bases so there is no room for doubt about what is expected. You need to ask:
- Were clear guidelines given?
- Were time frames realistic?
- Has the team member been given feedback?
- Does the team member have the ability to perform the job satisfactorily?
- What other options are left for improving poor performance?
- Has all reasonable support and encouragement been delivered from your end?

REGULAR FEEDBACK

If someone is not performing as they should, you need to flag it up quite quickly. Do not let things fester or linger – confront the issue and take action straightaway, using day-to-day notification, performance reviews, one-to-one chats, feedback through supervisors, etc. There is no point in ignoring problems in reviews or appraisals if you may later need to take disciplinary action.

You should feed back regularly to team members and understand that not doing so is as unfair to the employee as it is to you as an employer. Do not feel that you cannot point out issues as you go along – it is important, in the course of your day-to-day working lives, to embrace your responsibility to flag up matters to your team. This means you can be seen to behave in a fair and just manner with regard to your staff.

UNFAIR DISMISSAL

Current employment law states that employees have the right to take an employer to an industrial tribunal for unfair dismissal after 52 weeks' continuous service (however many days per week they work). This gives plenty of time – including trial periods – to address any concerns or raise any issues before longer-term employment begins. The exception to this 52-week rule is where discrimination is involved.

REASONS FOR DISCIPLINARY ACTION

There are three reasons for disciplinary action:
- poor performance
- misconduct
- gross misconduct.

It is helpful first to ascertain which area we are talking about or where the disciplinary procedure could be categorised.

POOR PERFORMANCE

When a member of the team is performing poorly, for instance, not providing adequate standards of work technically, you need to help them as much as possible to reach the required level of competence. It might be a customer-service-related issue, a technical concern or another matter which they could improve upon if given the time, help, training and education.

MISCONDUCT

Misconduct is defined as being an area where employees are not conducting themselves as the company requires. Examples of misconduct include: lateness, poor attendance, poor appearance, attitude problems, lack of motivation, rudeness to a customer, etc. If the employee knows what is expected of them, their misconduct needs to be pointed out as being unacceptable behaviour and action needs to be taken.

GROSS MISCONDUCT

Gross misconduct is often a situation which makes continuing with the employment untenable. It might be: misuse or theft of salon property, unauthorised periods of absence, substance abuse within working hours, etc. These would all be considered as instances of gross misconduct on the employee's behalf.

Once you have defined the area into which the problem falls, you need to further examine how to deal with it.

ANALYSING PERFORMANCE PROBLEMS

When looking at performance problems, I always ask myself: 'Could the employee do it if their life depended on it?' It is quite a good benchmark from which to judge a disciplinary situation. Use my 'analysing performance problems' chart to help you, for example:

- Could a graduate team member perform a complex colour change? Yes, over time and only if given the right training and education.
- Could a stylist be on time for work every day? Yes, if they wanted to.
- Could another employee ever deliver the right service levels after training and education? Possibly not – if they do not understand what you are trying to do within your team ethos, despite repeated feedback, training and education.

If there is a possible 'yes' answer, it is your duty and responsibility as an employer to guide, mentor, train and educate your team members to improve and correct the behaviour. If you are sure the employee cannot reach the required standard, it may be time to instigate disciplinary procedures and accept that the team member is not ever really going to be able to meet requirements – but only after all opportunities to improve have been exhausted. An employer should not be asking the impossible, for instance, a task which is not within the employee's job description to perform. But if the employee takes on a role which they are incapable of performing, or accepts a job which they are unable to do, they might be disciplined under poor performance if they are not doing it.

ANALYSING PERFORMANCE PROBLEMS

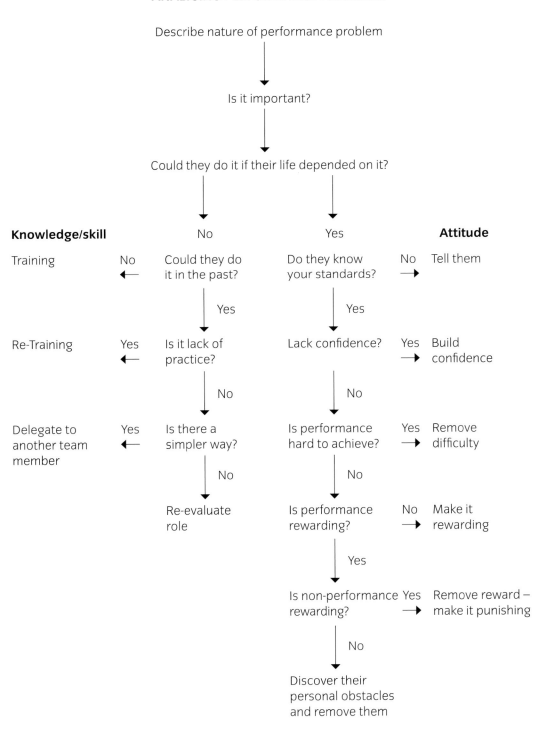

Describe nature of performance problem

Is it important?

Could they do it if their life depended on it?

Knowledge/skill   No   Yes   **Attitude**

Training   No ←   Could they do it in the past?   Do they know your standards?   No →   Tell them

Yes

Re-Training   Yes ←   Is it lack of practice?   Lack confidence?   Yes →   Build confidence

No

Delegate to another team member   Yes ←   Is there a simpler way?   Is performance hard to achieve?   Yes →   Remove difficulty

No

Re-evaluate role   Is performance rewarding?   No →   Make it rewarding

Yes

Is non-performance rewarding?   Yes →   Remove reward – make it punishing

No

Discover their personal obstacles and remove them

CREATING A DISCIPLINARY PROCEDURE AND GRIEVANCE POLICY

It is very much your duty to make employees aware of company rules and regulations; it is also your responsibility to make employees aware of company procedure and how it works. As salon managers, you need to make sure you have your own disciplinary procedure in place so the team know how the procedure will be instigated. They will be aware of what is defined in your rules and regulations as breaches of company policy that will require disciplinary action to be instigated.

In addition to this, you need to confirm how staff can deal with grievances that they might have. You should have a written procedure for how they can bring matters to the management's attention and how their concerns will be dealt with. Both the disciplinary procedure and grievance policy should be clearly displayed on your staff noticeboard and should form part of the terms and conditions of their employment.

Once your policies have been finalised, you need to ensure you are compliant with the **ACAS** Code of Practice (see below).

ACAS

(Advisory, Conciliation and Arbitration Service) exists to improve organisations and working life through better employment relations – see www. acas.org.uk

PERSONNEL FILES

I keep file notes on all of my team members. Each staff member has their own personnel file where I keep all relevant documents relating to them: holiday request forms, personal information, signed contracts of employment, etc. At the front I keep a file note form, where the relevant supervisors or managers or I can record notes about conversations that may later require disciplinary action. For instance, I record informal chats about lateness, performance, and so on, by stating the time, date, subject matter and a note of the conversation which took place and the initials of the manager or supervisor who mentioned the behaviour. This helps me to establish why I needed to start disciplinary procedure and acts as a good reminder, as well as a reference for the employee on the instances that might have led to a disciplinary interview.

ACAS CODE OF PRACTICE 2009

The conciliation body ACAS revised its Code and accompanying guidelines in 2009, following the Dispute Resolution Review. These are as follows:
- establish the key facts of the case
- inform the employee of the problem
- hold a meeting with the employee to discuss the problem
- allow the employee to be accompanied at the meeting
- decide on appropriate action
- provide employees with an opportunity to appeal.

More comprehensive advice and guidance on dealing with disciplinary and grievance situations is contained in the ACAS guidance booklet 'Discipline and Grievances at Work: The ACAS Guide' and is available for download from www.acas.org.uk

In essence, it is important to be fair. Do not ever let a situation get personal – keep it strictly professional and unemotional. During disciplinary procedures it is vital to keep a professional distance between yourself as a salon manager or owner and your team members. It is not advisable to socialise with your team one minute then have to discipline them the next and, above all, it confuses the relationship.

CONSTRUCTIVE DISMISSAL

This is the term used for a dismissal that is contrived unfairly – take all possible steps to avoid this. Keeping disciplinary procedure unemotional, factual, structured and in line with the ACAS code should ensure that it is being dealt with properly and professionally and without further implications or ramifications on your part.

INITIATING DISCIPLINARY PROCEDURE

In the first instance, you need to inform the team member that you will be holding a meeting to discuss a concern and that it may be of a disciplinary nature. You should not have decided what action you are going to take at this stage as it is essential for you to decide this only when you have heard the employee's comments after formally bringing it to their attention. It would be unfair if you had already decided on the action; even if you have a good idea of what action you might like to take, it is imperative that you get feedback from them before making up your mind.

Formal disciplinary meetings should be minuted and copies of these given to the employee.

Offer the employee a witness at this stage, and give them a time and date for the meeting. Then make sure you give them an idea of what the meeting is about, so they have time to consider their response. Do not go into detail at this stage; keep it so they have a rough idea of the nature of the meeting, such as failure to hit targets or poor attendance, etc.

POOR PERFORMANCE

Start the meeting by clarifying that the employee knows what is expected of them. Run through file notes to demonstrate how this has been communicated (when and how, verbally and by whom), and have job descriptions to hand to point out their areas of responsibility and demonstrate that you have been compliant in informing them what you expect from them.

In poor performances cases it is prudent to find out why the team member is not doing what is expected. Is it a training issue? Do they need role play, mentoring, or buddying? Find out the reasons why they have not been doing what is expected. Sometimes, they will not be able to give you a reason, which is perhaps most concerning. You need to dig and delve to uncover what is holding them back from delivering what you expect, especially if you are satisfied that they are fully aware of what they should be doing. It is your job to offer to help to resolve the matter. Inform them of the help that will be offered, how it will be offered and when.

FIRST AND SECOND STAGES

In the first instance, do this verbally but record dates and times in their staff file (you might think you will remember but, in all probability, you will not, so note it down). Give them a date on which you are going to review their performance (and stick to it).

At this second stage, if there is no or little improvement, it is probably time to start the official warning procedure with a verbal warning – recorded in writing.

OFFICIAL WARNING PROCEDURES

Once you decide to commence the warning procedure, following your meetings, issue:
- verbal warning
- followed by written warning
- then formal and final written warning.

Following the procedures

At every step of the way, you must follow the procedure. Let the employee know when and how you are going to consider the results of the disciplinary interview or hearing and what action may result. Let them know when the action will be taken, how, and by whom. Follow the steps: hold meetings at every stage and ensure that you ask how you can help them to resolve the issues. Discuss the matter in full. Give the employee time to improve. Put everything in writing, issue a review time and expiry time. Continue to record dates and times of any subsequent conversations, even if they are informal.

Offer them a witness at all levels. It is also wise to have a witness for yourself. The witness need not say anything; they are merely there to verify how the procedure was conducted. Ideally, the witness should have a supervisory or managerial role, or at the very least be a senior member of the team. The employee can have a witness of their choice and, if they choose another team member, you must not unreasonably deny time out of the workplace to attend such a meeting.

It may be prudent to get different managers or supervisors to carry out the separate hearings or procedures in the interest of absolute fairness.

Once the action has been decided on, confirm the decision in writing to the employee and detail the reasons for the action in your letter. Allow them to appeal against the action should they wish to, and keep them informed (in writing) of the next steps that will be taken.

TREATING UNRELATED DISCIPLINARY MATTERS SEPARATELY

Expiry times

Much will depend on the incident, but normally 3–12 months is adequate time to expect improvement and to leave a warning enforced for.

The warning procedure is usually only relevant to the incident it concerns. Once applied, it can stay in the employee's staff file past **expiry** for reference, but cannot be used as part of the disciplinary procedure. Remember the aim is to correct behaviour and turn around a situation. For instance, if you are going down a disciplinary route concerning poor work standards, and another issue arises, such as unauthorised absence, it is wise to start a fresh disciplinary procedure about the separate incident, rather than trying to dovetail two unrelated matters, which would not be deemed to be fair practice.

Example 1 Verbal Poor Performance

Dear Ms Stylist,

Following the disciplinary hearing attended by you this morning, this letter constitutes the verbal warning issued to you in accordance with the Company's Disciplinary Procedure. This Wearning concerns your poor performance regarding:

Unprofessional appearance for work – poor personal grooming, lack of make-up

As discussed with you on many previous occassions, it is essential for you to look groomed for work with clean, freshly pressed clothes, clean and groomed hair and wearing a light make-up. As pointed out to you on 1.3.12, 10.3.12 and again today your recent appearance has not been acceptable and does not comply with the company's standards. We have discussed in depth the areas where your appearance is not compliant.

As discussed, I have arranged some specialist make-up lesson training for you with one of our therapists to help you to further understand what is expected of you, the dates of which will be confirmed shortly.

Your performance will be reviewed in one month (on 13.4.12) by which time it is hoped that there has been a marked improvement. Should there not be an improvement by this time, you may be subject to further disciplinary procedure.

This warning will remain in force for 3 months (until 13.6.12)

You have the **right to appeal** against this disciplinary action within 5 days in accordance with the company's grievance procedure. Please put any appeal in writing to the attention of Ms Y.

Yours, etc.

Right of appeal

Your grievance procedure should include a right of appeal, so the employee has the chance to respond to any action they consider to be unfair.

MISCONDUCT

Misconduct is a more serious matter and may require more immediate action, depending on the severity of the issue. You do not necessarily have to go through the poor performance warning procedure of verbal, written, then formal and final written warning.

Some incidents will be serious enough to jump in at the relevant stage, and much will depend on the severity of the issue. Whatever the actual outcome of the disciplinary action taken, the steps and procedures must still be followed, so ensure you inform the employee of the disciplinary interview or hearing date, time and venue, allow them to have a witness, have a witness for yourself, and investigate and discuss the matter fully. Inform them of when you will call them back in to discuss the outcome of the meeting and what disciplinary action will be taken (if any). Once you have established the facts and decided on the action, allow them to appeal if they wish and keep them informed in writing every step of the way.

It may be necessary to suspend an employee over misconduct while the incident is being investigated. Notify the employee in writing about the suspension and the reasons for it. Suspensions are normally on full pay.

GROSS MISCONDUCT

Incidents of gross misconduct may immediately make employment untenable and you may move straight to a formal and final written warning, suspension or even dismissal, depending on the severity of the matter. However, whichever route you take, you must follow the correct steps by informing the employee of the meeting (even if the matter is so severe you have to hold it there and then, inform them of the nature of it before it commences). You should allow them to have a witness, arrange a witness for yourself and make sure you suspend and reconvene the meeting at a prearranged date and time to review the facts of the matter and discuss them, following full investigation. Once the disciplinary action has been decided, confirm the action in writing and state the case in full, detailing the reasons for your decision. Allow them to appeal against the action and state how and when the final salary will be paid, confirming their post-contractual obligations, should the outcome mean termination of their employment.

Example 2 Written Misconduct

Dear Ms Stylist,

Following our meeting today, where a disciplinary hearing was held, and despite your previous warnings on 12.9.12 where it was hoped there would be a significant improvement in your behaviour, this letter constitutes the formal written warning in accordance with the Company's Disciplinary Procedure regarding your misconduct in the following area:

Lateness on:
12.10.12 (10 mins), 13.10.12 (15 mins), 14.10.12 (20 mins) and 15.10.12 (15 mins)

This constant lateness is not satisfactory. On at least one occassion (14.10.12) your 9 am client was left waiting for 20 minutes and left the premises due to your lateness, resulting in a direct loss of business for both yourself and the company. This level of customer service from you is unacceptable.

It is hoped that this written warning will lead to a marked improvement in your time-keeping and that you will arrive at (or before) your start time of 8.45am as stated in your contract of employment from now on.

Your misconduct will be reviewed on 12.11.12 where it is hoped that there will be no need for further Disciplinary action. However, should there not be a marked improvement at that time, you may be subject to further action which may lead to your dismissal.

This warning will remain in force for 4 months (until 14.2.12).

You have the right to appeal against this disciplinary action within 5 days in accordance with the company's grievance procedure. Please put any appeal in writing to the attention of Ms Y.

Yours, etc.

Changing Behaviour

Even if the incident is severe and involves misconduct, ensure the employee is still given a full explanation of why the behaviour is unacceptable, and where this is pointed out in your employee handbook. Also confirm what instruction, guidance and training will be given to help resolve any issues.

SUMMARY

I am not an employment lawyer (and do not profess to be!) and this complex area needs proper specialist knowledge and advice for individual cases. But in describing the principles you need to consider, I can give you an overview of how to get the best results from your disciplinary procedures.

Remember, disciplinary procedure is about addressing issues and concerns to make changes that, it is hoped, will lead to a positive outcome for all concerned. It is not about being heavy handed or impetuous. It must be considered, detailed and precisely followed to obtain the best results. Whenever you are conducting disciplinaries, remember they should always be about correcting behaviour and amending performance so both you and your employee are moving in the right direction again. They are not a power struggle – so never treat them as such.

If in any doubt you should take expert legal advice.

CHAPTER 6
LEADERSHIP SKILLS

This chapter will look at the leadership skills you need to cultivate to be the most effective manager possible. We will cover how to get organised and manage your time, and the systems and techniques you can use to improve your managerial productivity. We will look at management styles, and how to delegate effectively. It will cover ways to keep yourself inspired and motivated, and the goals and plans you can set yourself. Finally, we will look at my 20 'golden management rules', devised from the many mistakes I have made over the course of my career, and what I have learned from each one!

QUALITIES OF A GOOD LEADER

A good leader has many qualities. He or she:

- is an efficient communicator
- has integrity and commitment
- is consistent
- gives great guidance
- encourages ideas and creative thinking
- is flexible and strategic
- is assertive and ambitious
- is determined and persuasive
- has confidence, vision and drive
- shows good judgement and diligence
- sets and achieves goals
- motivates and inspires
- and, above all, nurtures strengths, educates and develops areas of weakness.

PEOPLE SKILLS

A good leader adopts a proactive stance and can create a motivated atmosphere where people feel valued, praised and recognised. Whatever their management style, the team can feel that they are working with their manager towards a shared aim, rather than for them with little recognition.

A good manager and leader does not just manage a business, they are managing the team relationships within that business too – especially in our sector, which is so labour intensive and staff reliant – so they need to be patient, generous, empathetic and show sensitivity to others. To do this, they need to display a positive self-image and have the charisma to enable them to be a good role model and lead by example. They should always be the first to get their hands dirty. Above all, a great leader has big ears and a firm hand; they do not make assumptions and they show their team that they understand and respect them. They are not afraid to share knowledge and ask for help. They know it is not what you say, but how you say it that matters, and they take a genuine interest in their staff in every respect.

MANAGERS AND ENTREPENEURS

Entrepreneurs and managers can be an entirely different breed from each other and, while they tend to share some traits, overall they have different strengths. Entrepreneurs tend to have the 'just do it' mentality for creating ideas and developing strategies and often get bored by too much structure. Managers tend to achieve through others and have a more measured attitude to improving performance, assessing risks and translating strategy into action.

Most good managers are naturally 'team players' and live by the 'team' ethos:

Together
Everyone
Achieves
More

Team players have an ability to learn and absorb the skill sets of people around them and share knowledge and skills. The best team managers have a talent for working out which team member's skills are utilised best in which area, to enable everyone to contribute to the success of the business.

Good 'team-player' managers, therefore, will easily know their own attributes, and will have no problem in purposefully finding deputies or assistant managers or supervisors who have qualities that complement or make up for those that they may lack to create a balance of skill sets.

GETTING ORGANISED

Chaotic management is as uncomfortable for the manager as it is for the team member – nobody wants to work for someone who is constantly 'fire fighting' because they have not got their act together. Taking control of your time and prioritising tasks is a skill to be honed. Controlled management of your most precious resource (your time) is a sure way to help alleviate stress, too. To be as stress-free and efficient as possible, you need to sleep well, exercise, eat healthily, balance your work and social time and manage your working time effectively.

Being organised is an element of your leadership that your staff will respect you for – more than perhaps any other. People like routine, order, good practice and well-managed salons; they simply do not want to work in chaos. They require structure, efficiency and well-thought-out, carefully-planned systems that enable the operator to get on with their work without worry. It is not easy for operators who are running a busy column, and good staff will want to know that all the back-up systems are in place to let them get on with what they do best.

TIDY DESK, TIDY MIND

I really do think this saying is true. If your work space is orderly, structured and organised, with an office area that you can use for working, storing records, one-to-ones, interviews or meetings, and so on, and an in-tray of work you need to get through, with papers filed in neat, clearly-labelled files, you will automatically feel much more in control of your responsibilities. Your team will also like to see that everything is being looked after properly and taken care of well.

The three 'R's

So try to practise the three 'R's – read, respond and remove. Deal with things straightaway, then file them with notes written in pencil on the paperwork (for example, phoned back on x date, sent email on y date), so you have a reference point to refer back to and, most importantly, update. Never be afraid to make notes like this on paperwork – it is easy to think you will remember small details like this, but you will not and writing them down will help declutter your head. Have a regular clear-out – do not let things gather dust or become part of the furniture. Deal with them, file them, give them a home and adopt an 'out-of-sight, out-of-mind' thought process to keep your thinking clear.

TO-DO BOOKS

Keeping a book of lists is something I have always done. My 'to-do' list is updated at the end of the day for the next working day, and the tasks on it are ticked off as I go. Sometimes a task may stay on the list for a while, but eventually it will always get completed. Keeping a 'to-do' book is a great way of coping with stress, too. The act of writing the task down is crucial. It is psychologically proven that the act of transferring an issue to paper helps to mentally transfer it out of our minds, too. Ask other team members who have been given responsibility to keep a book or list, too, and then have a quick debrief to see where you are on particular tasks, when necessary.

Master 'to-do' list

It works well to create a master to-do list, with long-term objectives on it, and then do a sublist of daily tasks from this main list. For instance, your main to-do list might contain things like:

- rebranding the salon
- changing the staff uniform
- rewriting the company appraisal form
- refurbishing reception seating area.

Using the example above, for instance, focusing on the refurbishment of the reception seating area may be a red task or a task from your master list, but you could assign yourself aspects of the task, like looking at fabrics, paint or wallpaper for the reception area, as well as addressing your daily duties that need to be completed.

From this list of long-term objectives, you can also create time to address some of these tasks during the working day.

PRIORITISING 'TO-DO' LISTS

You can choose to prioritise these lists with a traffic light system and this works well for some managers. Green implies you have all the information you need to carry out the task, so it is given the status of 'go'; amber means you need further information and red flags up those that are going to be more of a problem. This allows you to carry out long-term improvements, so you can spend time looking at fabrics, paint or wallpaper for the reception area, as well as addressing your pressing daily duties.

Get into the habit of tackling the most difficult tasks and issues first thing in the morning, while you are fresh.

Daily tasks

Make sure you prioritise your daily tasks in order of importance.
So, your list might look like this:

- complete VAT returns
- do beauty stock order
- write back to interview applicant
- check staff holiday rota
- proofread new promotional signs
- rearrange retail area
- order light bulbs
- check paint swatches (master list).

Delegation

Then, see who can help you complete these tasks, using initials and names as a reference:

- complete VAT returns – HW
- do beauty stock order – head therapist/ HW to check
- write back to interview applicant – HW
- check staff holiday rota – head receptionist
- proofread new promotional signs – HW
- rearrange retail area – head junior
- order light bulbs – assistant manager
- check paint swatches (team feedback, as and when appropriate).

By delegating the tasks to different team members, and setting them a deadline of when you expect them to be completed (for example, by the end of the day, by the end of the week, etc) you can actually make your own tasks achievable. Above, HW is left with three tasks, and one to crosscheck. The team feedback tasks can be run by any free team member (helping them to feel involved) who HW comes across during the working day. Each of the other team members has one task only, and therefore the 'end of the day' goal is now achievable.

KEEPING A 'CAN-DO' ATTITUDE

It really is a fact that most of our successful entrepreneurs have a similar 'can-do' mentality. One common character trait they share is a 'just-do-it' attitude; they avoid procrastination and get things done quickly. Many have low boredom thresholds and know that the key to getting results is by getting on with it. Emulating this mindset is all-important to our success. High achievers simply do not dilly-dally, they 'do' instead, while others are still deciding. Adopting a 'get-it-done' attitude is therefore highly advisable.

They also have another common trait – they do not have a fear of failure. They often only talk about their successes but, invariably, they have failed at many ventures before everything has come together to result in success.

Fear of failure can hold you back, so try not to allow it to creep into your mentality. Visualise a positive outcome and use the power of positive thought to help you reach a solution. You can also use a technique called 'reframing' to put a positive spin on a problem and help you see it in a different light. There is often a positive side to a problem, if you look hard enough! I love the old saying, 'whether you think you can, or whether you think you can't, you're right on both counts'.

TIME MANAGEMENT

Managing your time effectively is a managerial skill you need to acquire. Remember, the Prime Minister only has the same number of hours in his day as you do – so making the time as productive as possible is the key. Learning how to multitask and how to cope with organising your time is essential to carrying out the many diverse aspects of your job; you will need to juggle your many roles and responsibilities and wear many different 'hats' as a salon manager. Good time management is about getting things done effectively and efficiently – using your time wisely and making sure your working day is as productive as possible.

MANAGERIAL TIME

Japanese business experts believe there are four types of managerial time:

- **operational time** (to correct past errors)
- **strategic time** (to plan for the future)
- **innovative time** (to become more competitive tomorrow)
- **kaizen time** (to make continuous improvements to ensure we will have a tomorrow).

They believe that no manager should spend more than 25% on operational issues and that the rest of the time should be divided between the remaining three categories in order to spend the optimum time working creatively.

MIND-MAPPING

Mind-mapping can be a useful exercise for dealing with problems. For instance, you can draw the shape of a tree and write the main part of the problem next to the larger branches, the smaller issues into smaller branches, and so on. This helps you to visualise which aspects you need to tackle individually rather than looking at the whole problem in one go. You could also try thought bubbles, or a ladder of priorities – whatever works for you.

(Source: *The Successful Manager's Handbook* by Moi Ali (DK)

DELEGATING

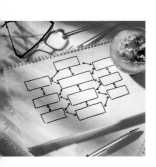

In our industry, it is important to remember that some, if not most, salon managers are working in smaller salons, where they are also running a column as a stylist, technician, therapist or nail technician, as well as dealing with their managerial responsibilities. It is, therefore, helpful to have a good deputy, and delegating some administrative tasks to a receptionist is inevitable. However, some things can only be done by you.

Salon managers who are working a column of clients often tell me that they simply do not have time to manage their salon effectively and service a successful and happy clientele, which is understandable. However, it simply is not an option to neglect the ever-growing, important responsibilities and duties that fall squarely upon your shoulders. So, it is really paramount that you give yourself the time to run your businesses effectively.

You should mark out at least one hour a day to get on top of your daily tasks, and give yourself at least one or two half-days to get on top of your work. I would advise small, regular chunks of time to attend to these matters, rather than marking yourself out one day a week for an office day. Keeping on top of things daily will make you feel more in control. Imagine only doing your laundry once a week, instead of as and when required – it is like facing a mountain of ironing (overwhelming and a bit depressing!). But ironing one shirt every day becomes manageable. It is the same with your workload. Unless you are willing to give yourself some (guilt-free!) time to actually focus on running the business, you simply will not be effective. You do not need to apologise for it, and you can educate your clients to understand when you are available for bookings and when you are not. Do not be tempted to take work home – you should not have to do this. If you do, something is wrong and you need to look again at your time management.

WORK–LIFE BALANCE

Some salon managers I know overcompensate for their management or office time by then working an extra day on the floor. You should not need to do this. Putting in a good, productive five-day week is sufficient – you should not exhaust yourself in the belief that only you can look after your clients or they will leave you. They will not – encourage them to try other operators if you are not available, and try not to compromise on your management time.

Most operators I know remain insecure and worry about their popularity – whatever level they are working at! No doubt, if you are running a column too, you will have an inbuilt fear of losing clients and worry about taking time to attend to managerial tasks and the effect this will have on your clientele. Try not to!

ACCOMPLISHMENT

At the end of every day, remind yourself of what you have accomplished. Research suggests this is excellent for our happiness levels and work enjoyment. When you are tired, or your nerves are frazzled, this helps you to realise how effective you have been. This feeling of having achieved something is motivating and inspiring and fits in perfectly with my 'setting bite-sized goals' theory (and also validating your time off the salon floor, if you are running a column, too!).

EMAILS

Emails can be a blessing and a curse. Sometimes, they are brilliant for increasing efficiency and getting things done quickly, but sometimes, when time is being managed ultra-carefully, they can be a real distraction. Manage your email by deleting junk items every day and creating a 'follow-up' folder in your inbox. Then go back to your follow-up folder when time allows and respond to emails in order of priority so you do not feel swamped. If you want to get important tasks done, make sure you complete these before checking emails.

Make sure to give yourself some designated 'email checking' time every day, but you should not prioritise emails over completing tasks.

PHONE CALLS

The most efficient people I know do not allow phone calls to 'eat into' their structured time, and take phone calls only if and when it suits them – getting messages and calling back instead. If you set aside an hour to get through a task, try not to be distracted if the phone rings and do not spend the time with your ear glued to your mobile. Compartmentalise your time so that you have time for tasks, time for phone calls, time for meetings and so on, and learn to be quite strict with yourself. Otherwise, you can end up being a very busy fool but getting nothing done.

HOW TO HOLD EFFICIENT MEETINGS

There are some pointers to remember regarding the efficiency of meetings.

What to do

Try to make sure you do the following.

- Have a meeting objective. Do not have a meeting just for the sake of it. If you're not careful, your day can be forever spent having meetings and not getting things done!
- Be punctual. It is really important.
- Make notes on the time, date, who is present, what the objective of the meeting is, who has to follow up on what and by when. File these notes away once the tasks are complete; but leave them in the in-tray until such time, to remind you of what still needs to happen.
- Follow-up any issues in an email, unless you are the customer – when they should follow-up to you. People can be very lax in this area and it smacks of unprofessionalism; be firm with people who cannot be bothered to follow-up but who want your business.
- Set a time frame by which the meeting should be finished. Avoid lunchtime meetings when eating/hunger can get in the way.
- Make sure the meeting is uninterrupted, if possible.

What not to do

You should try to avoid the following.

- A meeting with anyone who has not brought a pen and paper with them. Offer them one if they do not have one. In my experience, if they do not bother to write anything down, they are going to be relying on you to remind them. Refuse to do this – particularly if they are a supplier and you are their customer.
- Booking meetings by email. You can end up playing 'email ping-pong' when it is easier and quicker to pick up the phone to arrange.

Day, not just date!

In meetings, and for other notes, get into the habit of writing the day of the week as well as the date – so Wednesday 13 June rather than just 13th June. It will increase your efficiency just by saving any potential misunderstandings – particularly in February, which in a non-leap year has the same days and dates as March.

MANAGEMENT STYLES

Ultimately, to succeed in the hairdressing and beauty industry, you need to be a people person; someone who enjoys being with people. To get intrinsic job satisfaction, you not only need to be a good communicator, but a great empathiser and motivator. Above all, you must show consistency in your management approach so your team knows where they are with you. Being hot headed, impetuous or liable to fly off the handle one minute and then serious and professional the next is no good. You need to aim for consistency in order to make your team feel secure. Nobody wants a manager who is their best friend one minute and a harridan the next.

There are, many different styles of management. You will create a blend of characteristics that is unique for you. However, I would urge that you make consistency your priority. What you want to avoid at all costs is a lack of decision making (or, worse, continually changing your mind). People respond particularly badly to this. Firm, fair decisions are crucial to your integrity.

DIFFERENT MANAGEMENT STYLES

There are several management styles.

Autocratic

This style of manager is dominant. Autocratic managers like to make decisions alone and without consultation. They can be controlling and make unilateral (affecting all) decisions without regard for team members, so decisions are often made without consultation. This can create an image of a well-managed business, but can conversely encourage team members to require more supervision and encourage dependency on the manager. Autocratic leaders can either be directive (controlling of team members) or permissive (giving leeway to the team members in carrying out their work).

Paternalistic

The paternalistic style can also be dictatorial. However, this type of leader takes the best interest of the employees into account, and the role becomes more pastoral (socially aware) and paternal (fatherly or parental), as the manager listens to opinions but still makes the decisions. Communication is generally downward, but feedback is encouraged.

Democratic

Democratic managers believe in consultation and actively encourage the sharing of ideas among the group. They tend to ask for opinions, giving employees a chance to share their views and therefore allowing them to take part in the decision-making process, entering into extensive communication with them. They believe in individual empowerment. Staff are allowed to complete the task in their own manner, but deadlines and goals must be met – encouraging a sense of belonging. Some team members can take advantage of this style, as it is heavy on delegation and encourages ownership of tasks set. (This is definitely my favoured style.)

Laissez-faire

'Laissez-faire' literally means 'leave to do'. This type of manager evades conventional management duties by setting tasks and giving staff freedom to complete tasks when they see fit, encouraging unco-ordinated delegation. It can work well in creative environments, but often results in a lack of staff focus and direction; this results in dissatisfaction from team members, as the style is more of a coaching role and team members can feel a little 'lost'. Many salon managers who are also busy running columns fall into this category.

Consultative

Consultative managers can be a combination of autocratic and democratic, and probably strike a good balance between the two styles.

Your own management style will naturally develop and become a combination of some of the above. It is worth trying to develop a more democratic style, as I have always found that empowering people to make their own decisions creates a determination for the task to succeed and, therefore, can produce successful results.

MANAGEMENT TECHNIQUES

In addition to different management styles, there are some management techniques that you will find helpful.

BRAINSTORMING

This is an extremely useful process – otherwise known as team creative thinking. Whereas rational thinking is a logical process, creative thinking challenges the team to think laterally. The brainstorming process throws creative thinking open to the team as a whole to think 'out of the box'. It can inspire probing questions to provoke different perspectives and help people to come up with new ideas. Harnessing the power of our (naturally creative) teams to help us think up new innovations is a worthwhile task and one which I find teams enjoy.

BEING DILIGENT

Very often, as a manager, you will be put on the spot. Sometimes, staff, customers and business associates, will throw you a 'curve ball' and ask you a difficult question or one you do not know the answer to. I have learned to say 'let me get back to you on that'; I then go off and do the research, replying once I know the facts. Nobody minds, as long as you do remember to get back to them (without a prompt, if you want to look efficient).

DELEGATION

A good manager is essentially one whose business runs as well when they are not there as it does when they are. This is your aim. However, it is not easy to achieve and is certainly impossible unless you are good at delegating.

Good delegation is about watching, observing and noting who is good at doing what, then issuing bite-sized tasks to other team members to conduct on your behalf. A good delegator cannot be a control freak – you have to let people find the way of doing things that works for them and be prepared to let them makes some mistakes. Observe their ability to carry out the task, then input into offering some advice to help them do it better next time. Do not fall into the trap of saying 'Oh well, I might as well do it myself'. Change will never happen that way.

Nurturing people

For example, you might find a salon junior is showing real ability and responsibility for looking after the retail area, so notice this and then empower them to be in charge of merchandising. Tell them how often you want them to rearrange the displays, and what they need to do on a daily basis, such as restocking the shelves. Then let them get on with it, advising them to come and get you for your input regularly. Tell them what they have done well, and explain gently what they could do better. But, critically, do not do it for them. Let them do it again, with concise reasons and instructions for why it was not quite right first time around. That way, they become more efficient, the task becomes one you can remove from your duties, and you can involve them in taking a managerial responsibility, however small.

Delegation makes people feel like they really belong, and frees up your time for things that really cannot be done by anyone but you.

Spending your time finding people to nurture in this way is a wise use of your time and resources. Not only does it get everyone 'on side' and thinking in the right way (that is, for the good of the business), but people like to be trusted and given responsibility. Above all, people thrive off feeling involved and that their contribution to the success of the salon is valued. It might be a small task, such as putting someone in charge of ordering the loo rolls, but it really does bring a team together and make them feel that they are doing it *with* you and not *for* you.

A good delegator communicates the tasks well, teaches and trains the way they want things performed – then empowers people to get on with it, without interference, reviewing what has been done and encouraging better performance next time.

Learning to let go is not easy. Think of it like watching a small child ride a bike for the first time. Nothing can compare with letting them just get on with it and learning from their mistakes. If they fall, you have to watch them get up, dust themselves down and carry on – a good metaphor for our managerial aims.

APPOINTING A NUMBER TWO

Finding a good assistant or deputy who you can effectively delegate to is essential. When you spot potential in a member of staff, start by giving them a small task which requires a bit of 'out-of-the-box' thinking to see if they are on your wavelength. If your relationship with your number two is going to work well, they really must think as you do. Remember, talent can be hidden anywhere – so always be on the lookout for people whose skills you can cultivate. You are ideally looking for someone who can help you look for solutions rather than point out problems, and who will help you listen to your own instincts (and theirs) when making difficult decisions.

WALT DISNEY'S STRATEGY

Walt Disney had a famous strategy in his management style. His philosophy was to integrate creative and logical thinking by making sure each meeting had three elements – a dreamer, a realist and a critic, with each thinker playing a different role. The dreamer is the visionary, the realist will take the concept and think about it practically, and the critic will think logically and cautiously. This can create a perfect soundboard and balance of three very different but very valuable skills.

PERL CYCLE FOR EFFECTIVE MANAGEMENT

The four stages of the PERL cycle allow you to learn from experience: Plan – Execute – Reflect – Learn.
- **P**lan – get into the habit of planning actions thoroughly.
- **E**xecute – carry out the plan and adapt it if necessary.
- **R**eflect – think about how you could improve processes in the future.
- **L**earn – make sure you learn lessons from your past actions.

Going through the process helps you to work out how you are going to achieve an objective, make sure you keep your focus on it, then assess the implications of all your actions and, finally, look at procedures you could change. It helps you to avoid the repetition of mistakes and the recurrence of problems.

(Source: *The Successful Manager's Handbook* by Moi Ali (DK)

WHO MOTIVATES THE MOTIVATOR?

As a salon owner or manager, there will be few individuals with whom you can share the burden of responsibility. Delegating is all very well, but confiding in others about worries and problems is much harder; so cultivating a good deputy is essential. It really does pay to attend courses and seminars aimed at a business level within the sector, not only to learn and keep evolving your skills, but to meet and share with other salon managers. When I conduct my business education, salon managers get as much out of this element as they do from the education itself.

Regularly training yourself is vital to ensure you remain focused and up to date with innovations and technologies but, above all, to keep you feeling fresh, motivated and inspired in such a challenging role. Try to attend either a training course, networking event or other such seminar at least once a year, but ideally every six months.

WHAT NEXT?

It is a good idea to have a plan for the future. It may be that you are managing a salon for someone else, and the natural progression is to open your own business. It may be that you are perfectly happy in your role, but perhaps you need an incentive to keep you focused, like having a bonus that is structured around the salon's profitability so you have a share in the success you have helped to create, or being involved with the company's expansion by helping to open other salons and develop a more senior managerial role.

If you are already a salon owner, it may be prudent to start thinking about your own exit plans. Hair and beauty salons are not particularly sellable; they are a uniquely labour intensive business and most investors will not invest in people, preferring to invest in tangible assets, like products or less personal retailers. However, management buyouts and takeovers from senior staff are more common in our sector, so it may be that if you as an owner have had enough, it is time to see if your workforce, or individuals within it, might want to take over the reins.

20 GOLDEN RULES

Over the years, I have made lots of mistakes as I have learned my profession and developed my skills. Remember, we choose to be managers, so we must always set the example. Here are my 20 'golden rules', based on that experience.

1 **Plan, plan, plan**
Fail to prepare, prepare to fail! Prepare for a rainy day, both emotionally and financially. There will be good times and bad.

2 **Be a pessimist/realist**
You can only be pleasantly surprised! Save too much for tax and over-budget to allow for unforeseen circumstances.

3 **Get back to basics**
Spend a day as a junior and see where your systems fall down. Get back to the floor regularly to see things as your team do, and act on what you find out.

4 **Bosses must be perfect**
Unfortunate but true – be there (minimal sickness), be fair, be punctual, be orderly, be organised, give good client care, always set an example, be consistent, look good.

5 **The 80/20 rule**
You will spend 80% of your time on 20% of your staff. Look after the 'plodders' – they are essential too.

6 **Nip nasty atmospheres in the bud**
Hold appraisals and regular staff meetings to clear the air. Find out if there is a bad apple or non-team player, then act.

7 **Expect to make unpopular decisions**
Do not expect to be everybody's friend – it is impossible. Be fair. Do not let emotion cloud decisions or affect your judgement. Your team do not want you as their friend, so avoid excessive socialising with them.

8 **Be diligent**
Keep a 'to-do' book and always get back to people – do not make them remind you. Remember, it may have taken a great deal of courage to ask you in the first place.

9 **Confront problems**
Do not be an ostrich and bury your head in the sand – embrace the dilemma and it will not feel so overwhelming. Do not procrastinate – make decisions and stick to them. Be objective and do not be afraid to get tough.

10 **Delegate and teach**
Communicate your way to your team. Never stop hammering the message home in order to get your team to share your vision.

11 Praise – criticise – praise
Always leave staff on a positive note – learn how to deliver the 'crap' sandwich (!) so your team can concentrate on improving the bad bits and are motivated by how well they are doing.

12 Believe in yourself
Nothing worthwhile is ever easy. Remember Thomas Edison's words when asked how it felt to have failed at his invention of the electric light: "I haven't failed 700 times, I've found 700 ways that don't work. When I find the way that does, I'll let you know." Learn to develop a 'can-do' attitude.

13 Everything is your problem and your responsibility
This seems overwhelming, but is true. From a dud light bulb, to a bad customer experience; it is all down to you.

14 Clear your head
If it gets too much, walk round the block – calm down. It won't seem so bad when you go back. Take time out. Do not take work home with you. Manage your time effectively.

15 Keep a bedside notebook
Write things down to clear your thoughts – sleep on any tough decisions. Your head will always feel clearer in the morning.

16 Beware of people who can deliver miracles!
There are no miracle cures – find the way of working that suits you, and avoid the 'do it this way' approach from people who should spend more time concentrating on what they are doing themselves. Listen to people who have actually done something – not those who make a living talking about doing it.

17 Stay focused
Be sure you can cope with growing and evolving; expansion can mean diluting success. Do not over-reach yourself. Get your people in place and delegate well before trying to expand.

18 Expect the curve balls
Someone will always throw you a curve ball when you are least expecting it. Do not expect your job to be stress-free. Feeling cocky normally equals impending disaster.

19 Learn – unlearn – relearn
Richard Branson says he's learned more from his failures than his successes. Pick yourself up, dust yourself down and start all over again, just as the song goes.

20 Take your team on the journey with you
Your staff will not want to hear about your stress or workload, and they equally do not expect you to be flash. Be humble and people will warm to you, and want to do it with you, not for you.

SUMMARY

Getting into the swing of good management practice through delegation, time management and strong leadership will always produce results. It is no good being spot-on with the finances if you are hopeless with people. We are a people business so your people skills are the most precious tool to hone – relating to, dealing with, empowering, motivating and communicating well with our teams and our customers is all a skill set we should all concentrate on developing.

Being efficient and consistent are the critical elements. If you want to be the boss, you simply cannot be everyone's friend. You are not there to win a popularity contest; that is not what your team want from you. They want leadership, inspiration, guidance and direction, delivered in an empathetic manner; but, above all, they want consistency, structure and good order. Cultivate this approach, and try to emulate a democratic or consultative managerial style, and you will be a great manager.

PART 2
INTRODUCTION:
MONITORING
FINANCIAL TEAM
PERFORMANCE

Now you have developed your 'dream team', you need to look at ways to get the most out of their performance – for their benefit and that of the salon. You do not need to apologise for the fact that you are in business to make money – in fact, your staff must learn to be as focused on seeing their column as a business as you are as salon owners and managers. In many respects, this section is the most critical for you to adopt – as the systems and procedures I recommend will inevitably translate into your business success.

This second part of the book will cover the systems and practices that I have used for more than two decades to ensure all of the team are delivering individually, and consider how we can maximise what we essentially sell – time and expertise.

We will look at the KPIs (key performance indicators) that you will need to track on an individual basis to help your operators think commercially about their clienteles. These will help you create a benchmark in your salons for your team to aspire to. We will also look at what you need to track and monitor – as well as how to do it.

We will look at how you can incentivise your team financially for optimum results and how to evaluate their performance through structured appraisals. We will also cover how to conduct a proper appraisal and what you need to be analysing during it. We will look at the competitions and incentives you can use to optimise their turnover and track and monitor their takings to get the best results, with tips to get the best results all round. Then, most importantly, we will cover how to retain your key operators and ensure your staff turnover is as low as possible, through creating career paths and ensuring you maximise on the diversity of your operators' skill sets.

Finally, this section looks at the booking systems and procedures you can establish to maximise that most valuable commodity – your appointment times. What we sell is time; so using tried-and-tested methods to maximise and sell your time wisely is crucial to your financial performance, and is a mindset to be created and encouraged throughout your whole team.

CHAPTER 7
INDIVIDUAL PERFORMANCE

This chapter will look at how to maximise productivity and performance on an individual level. We will look at what the benchmarks should be, and how to create your own, as well as the KPIs (key performance indicators) that are industry-standard. We will cover how to develop a salon ethos of the team running their columns as if they were their own businesses, to deliver maximum productivity for them and profitability for you, as well as which poor performance signs to look for.

CREATING YOUR DREAM TEAM

Ideally, your dream team will be monitored through regular appraisal and evaluation, and your team members will be nourished and nurtured. They will know what is expected of them because they have both job descriptions and clear financial targets, and you will reward excellence and act on poor performance. You will set and maintain consistent standards through a good example, and will grow our own team as they will prove to be the most loyal; and, if you invest in their training, they will ultimately be the best. But while that all sounds simple in theory, you need to put some procedures and structures in place in order to monitor your progress towards these goals and put them into practice.

WORKING SMART AND NOT HARD

Ideally, everyone should all use their time so efficiently and value every hour of the day so as to maximise and optimise time in the most financially beneficial way possible. Encouraging an ethos of working smart and not hard is essential to getting the most out of your teams. Traditionally, hairdressers, technicians, therapists and nail technicians work around their clients, taking breaks to fit in around their customers' schedules and the demands on their time, valuing the bookings and putting their needs on the back burner for the benefit of a busy column. This working arrangement requires a certain degree of flexibility on both sides; when the operator is not busy they may sit in the staff area or pop out, but there are times when lunch will be a grabbed sandwich between clients. Marking out breaks in their days only serves to limit potential appointment bookings and restrict productivity; but if the team work hard then you, as a manager, should be flexible in allowing them to go home early or even come in a bit later if they have worked through their breaks.

If you do not develop this approach, it can seriously affect your productivity. Some team members may challenge you about working in this manner, but remember that if they want official breaks marked out they will also have to be working when they are not busy (and sitting in the staffroom may not count) so normally a healthy status quo develops where the operator ends up getting all their entitled rest periods but opts to take them at a time to suit the business.

PERFORMANCE LEAGUES

Embracing the need for transparency in the financial elements of the business, a performance league is a great idea. It seems to me rather archaic for salon managers not to want to share financial information and communicate it to their team. There is nothing wrong with everybody, even your trainees, knowing the numbers you are after in order to remain profitable and stay secure and safe; so do not be alarmed about sharing information on who is doing what financially.

Rewarding performance

Every week, pin up a spreadsheet demonstrating who has done what in the business and then reward good performance and monitor success. These leagues are not only a great motivational tool, but they help to develop a healthy work ethic and positive attitude to financial success; they also help to cement the KPIs that you are tracking. (See Book 2 Chapter 3 for more detail on KPIs.)

Performance leagues encourage healthy competition in a positive way and they give the team a good insight into staff performance on a weekly basis so they can see how well they have done or which areas need improvement; in turn, this helps them to achieve their targets. They also work particularly well to track incentives and promotional performance. They can help to establish a hierarchy of positions so that other team members can see not only how they are performing, but how they are performing in comparison with their peers. Highlight any areas where the performance targets have been reached, and comment on and praise any outstanding achievements.

As with all systems, you cannot ask for consistency from your teams if you do not deliver it yourself so make sure, if you start something like this, that it is done regularly and without fail.

As well as tracking the KPIs (see below), make sure you list:

- how many days worked for each operator
- the number of new clients
- the number of request clients
- total number of clients.

Also track referral figures if you have them; this helps you to see who is link-selling, or even up-selling, and cross-referring to other departments and colleagues.

There's a multitude of things to look at. For example, for operators conducting multiple services you could break down the percentage of total treatments by the relevant service (ie technical as a percentage of total hairdressing services or manicure as a percentage of overall treatments) by operator too.

Whatever you decide to monitor, for the sake of continuity, you should keep the figures you are tracking the same each week. This will help to encourage a real understanding among your teams of what they are going to be assessed on during their appraisals.

Weekly takings

W/E 23.7.11

HAIR	days	ACTUAL	TARGET	(+/-)	CH	MISC	TOTAL	TARGET	(+/-)	REGS	TRAN	TOTAL CLIENTS	% REQ	AV.BILL	% OCC.	Email Cards	TECHNICAL	TARGET
Franco	4	£2,571.40	£3,000.00	-428.60	£0.00	£216.50	£216.50	£300.00	-83.50	24	1	25	96.0%	£102.86	63.3		£1,060.00	£1,200.00
Karen	0	£0.00	£2,300.00	-2,300.00	£0.00	£0.00	£0.00	£230.00	-230.00	0	0	0	#DIV/0!	#DIV/0!	0.0		£0.00	£920.00
Amanda	5	£2,483.95	£2,300.00	183.95	£7.00	£203.50	£210.50	£230.00	-19.50	23	8	31	74.2%	£80.13	65.6		£1,295.00	£920.00
Belinda	5	£2,223.00	£2,300.00	-77.00	£0.00	£80.75	£80.75	£230.00	-149.25	25	4	29	86.2%	£76.66	68.1		£695.00	£920.00
Samantha	5	£1,592.80	£1,800.00	-207.20	£7.00	£53.00	£60.00	£180.00	-120.00	21	4	25	84.0%	£63.71	52.2		£875.00	£720.00
Eddie	4	£1,449.90	£1,400.00	49.90	£0.00	£139.30	£139.30	£140.00	-0.70	17	5	22	77.3%	£65.90	67.2		£427.50	£560.00
Sunjay	5	£1,998.14	£1,500.00	498.14	£0.00	£40.00	£40.00	£150.00	-110.00	24	11	35	68.6%	£57.09	72.0		£2,236.25	£600.00
James	5	£1,914.44	£1,300.00	614.44	£0.00	£85.00	£85.00	£130.00	-45.00	27	5	32	84.4%	£59.83	68.3		£1,298.00	£520.00
Diana	5	£1,735.50	£800.00	935.50	£0.00	£0.00	£0.00	£80.00	-80.00	28	7	35	80.0%	£49.59	63.9		£1,090.00	£320.00
Jemal	5	£1,156.00	£800.00	356.00	£0.00	£79.00	£79.00	£80.00	-1.00	23	11	34	67.6%	£34.00	65.0		£1,865.00	£320.00
Tim	4	£1,188.00	£800.00	388.00	£0.00	£66.50	£66.50	£80.00	-13.50	21	8	29	72.4%	£40.97	56.0		£1,820.00	£320.00
COLOUR	days	ACTUAL	TARGET	(+/-)	CH	MISC	TOTAL	TARGET	(+/-)	REGS	TRAN	TOTAL CLIENTS	% REQ	AV.BILL				
Kathy	5	£3,225.00	£3,000.00	225.00	£0.00	£59.00	£59.00	£300.00	-241.00	22	5	27	81.5%	£119.44	61.3			
Sonia	5	£3,076.25	£3,000.00	76.25	£0.00	£0.00	£0.00	£300.00	-300.00	16	9	25	64.0%	£123.05	56.7			
David	5	£3,691.25	£3,000.00	691.25	£0.00	£81.75	£81.75	£300.00	-218.25	26	3	29	89.7%	£127.28	70.7			
Louisa	5	£2,160.00	£2,000.00	160.00	£0.00	£0.00	£0.00	£200.00	-200.00	25	6	31	80.6%	£69.68	59.4			
Sally	5	£1,736.25	£2,000.00	-263.75	£0.00	£107.90	£107.90	£200.00	-92.10	13	4	17	76.5%	£102.13	55.6			
MANICURE	days	ACTUAL	TARGET	(+/-)	CH	MISC	TOTAL	TARGET	(+/-)	REGS	TRAN	TOTAL CLIENTS	% REQ	AV.BILL				
Tina	0	£0.00	£1,100.00	-1,100.00	£0.00	£0.00	£0.00	£110.00	-110.00	0	0	0	#DIV/0!	#DIV/0!	0.0			
BEAUTY	days	ACTUAL	TARGET	(+/-)	CH	MISC	TOTAL	TARGET	(+/-)	REGS	TRAN	TOTAL CLIENTS	% REQ	AV.BILL				
Gemma	5	£1,949.48	£1,500.00	449.48	£0.00	£131.00	£131.00	£300.00	-169.00	12	12	24	50.0%	£81.23	82.1			
Mary	5	£1,666.80	£1,700.00	-33.20	£0.00	£891.50	£891.50	£340.00	551.50	14	24	38	36.8%	£43.86	73.9			
Brittany	5	£1,670.49	£1,700.00	-29.51	£0.00	£44.00	£44.00	£340.00	-296.00	17	10	27	63.0%	£61.87	78.9			
Beauty desk					£0.00	£20.00	£20.00	£200.00	-180.00									
MISC.		ACTUAL	TARGET	(+/-)	CH	MISC	TOTAL	TARGET	(+/-)									
Juniors		£365.50	£300.00	65.50	£0.00	£1,060.45	£1,060.45	£300.00	760.45									
Desk takings		£0.00	£300.00	-300.00	£190.00	£3,272.20	£3,462.20	£2,000.00	1,462.20									

Jr Name	Takings/ Retail
Karl	£124.50
Lee	£169.20
Catherine	£55.00
Sabrina	£145.00
Elle	£20.00

View online or download at www.cityandguilds.com/USM

KPIs

There are multiple things you can track and monitor with your teams, but I consider the most vital to be those shown below. If I track these five key elements, I can pretty much assess any team member simply by looking at the figures:

1 turnover
2 retail sales
3 percentage request
4 occupancy rate
5 average bill.

TURNOVER

Turnover denotes what part team members play in the success of the business and, as such, is vital. Always show weekly figures, so they can get a real feel for their performance. Show turnover in gross, as employees do not generally understand VAT liabilities. However, you can show the net figure alongside for information purposes and to help them calculate their commission. Group similar operators from the same tier/price level together on the league so that, indirectly, they get used to assessing and comparing their performance against their peers. These figures should be easy to calculate, either from your software, or by breaking down your turnover into the individual's performance every day and adding up the total for the week. Show the percentage plus or minus against the target figure too.

RETAIL SALES

Show each operator's total weekly retail sales alongside their target, along with the percentage plus or minus against target. Remember, this should be 10% of the total turnover, ideally. Again, obtain this information by getting a daily breakdown of performance and then adding up the week's total, either manually or using a software system.

PERCENTAGE REQUEST

Perhaps the single most important KPI is the percentage of customers who requested to rebook with the operator. Shown as a percentage of their total number of customers, this is one vital statistic on which operators should get used to being benchmarked. It is not an indication of financial success – remember that someone who only does one client a day could be on 100% if that client requested the operator! However, it will, when viewed along with turnover, be the most potent indicator of performance.

It is essential to monitor, using your booking system, which clients requested each operator, and which are considered to be new or transient. A transient client can be a regular salon client who simply does not mind who they see. This type of client should not be recorded as a request. Only deem a client to be a request client if they actually ask for their operator by name. To calculate percentage request manually, simply add up the total number of clients overall, and then find out the number of request clients and express as a percentage.

Example

Naomi does 10 clients in a day: eight of them have requested her by name – one is new to the salon and one is the client of another operator who is sick and has not specifically requested Naomi. That day, therefore, she is running at 80% request.

To calculate this as a percentage for the whole week, simply divide the request clients by the total clients, and press the percentage button on your calculator. So, if Naomi had 39 request clients out of a total of 52, enter 39 divided by 52 and press the percentage button, then the equals button to find out that her request rate was 75% for that week.

Benchmark request rate

I would expect that a good operator on any level should be able to reach 70% request after one year's continuous employment, and they should be hitting 50% after six months. Failure to hit these figures would ring warning bells – remember that, even at 70%, we are accepting that three out of 10 customers, or 30%, do not want to rebook the operator, which may result in three out of 10 customers not returning to the salon at all.

The dangers of too high a request rate

More senior team members will normally be high in their percentage request (high 80s, low 90s even), and younger, less established team members might be only slightly under this figure, performance-wise. But it is wise to make sure that percentage requests do not go too high as this can mean a lack of new clients into the operator's client base. Bearing in mind there is a natural shedding of clients (people move away, naturally leave, etc) an established operator will need constant replenishment of their clientele, not only to optimise their increased tariff, but also to keep their earning potential maximised.

OCCUPANCY RATE

Although it is harder to calculate (in that it is not usually tracked by a lot of software systems), occupancy rate is equally important, as it really analyses the productivity of your operators. You can simply work it out manually by calculating the number of possible productive hours, and expressing the total time booked with appointments as a percentage of the total productive time available, using the same principle as above. Try to work it out daily and average out across the week to get a total for your weekly performance league. Keep track of these totals to get figures for reviews and appraisals or for six-monthly performance leagues.

Example

So, if an operator had 40 hours' productive time available, of which 25 hours were booked, enter 25 divided by 40 and press the percentage button and then the equals button, to find out that her occupancy rate was 62.5%.

Benchmark occupancy rate

I would aim for 70% occupancy rate across all levels of operator, regardless of their experience tier or price level, after one year's continuous employment. After six months' employment, I would be looking for a 50% occupancy rate. I calculate this without taking breaks into consideration, as I aim for all operators to be achieving these rates and having a 'give and take' attitude to their working day. Remember, even at the 70% benchmark, nearly a third of their day is empty so this should allow for plenty of breaks and, more importantly, for lots of up-selling opportunities.

AVERAGE BILL

The customer's average bill or spend is calculated by simply dividing an operator's total turnover by the overall number of customers seen during a day, or week. So, if an operator generated £1000 gross turnover in a week, and had 40 clients, the average bill is £25 (or £20.83 net of VAT). Revisit Book 1 Chapter 3 for more detail on VAT.

The average spend will, of course, depend on the tariff or price tier of the operator; but by calculating it, you can work to improve the customer's average bill by educating and training on up-selling techniques and the link-selling of services.

TARGETS

According to experience tier/level and price banding, you can assess what you hope to expect of any operator, on any level, financially. This target should be set annually (at a minimum, or six-monthly at a maximum) at appraisal, and monitored throughout the year via the performance league. If an operator goes up a tier or level, the target of course will be reset as appropriate. You can break down the target into separate services if you choose, but make sure you do not make it too confusing. It should always be broken down into a daily target, with a retail amount also targeted weekly and broken down daily. Again, keep figures in gross so employees can understand it more easily.

Example

For instance, a senior stylist might have a £1000.00 weekly target (gross), which across five days works out at £200 per day. If the average bill target is £50, she needs to see four clients per day. The retail sales target might be £100 per week (10% of target figure), which across five days works out at £20 per day (2 x products @ £10 average product price).

Therefore, this operator knows that if she sees at least four clients per day and retails a product to two of them, she will hit her target. This is far simpler for her to understand and achieve when broken down in this manner.

CHAMPAGNE TARGETS

In addition to the targets set above, have an inspirational target for exceptional performance which, assessed weekly, means the operator wins a bottle of champagne (or something similar) from the company to reward this special result. For instance, using the example above, this operator's champagne target might be £1300, a 30% increase on her regular targeted performance.

INDIVIDUAL PERCENTAGE PAYROLL COSTS

With payroll being your biggest expense, and also being a variable cost, it is worth making sure you keep your individual employee costs in line. You can do this by regularly assessing (at each pay period) the total gross pay of the individual (including all PAYE and NICs – the true cost to the company) as a percentage of their net turnover (less VAT) over the pay period. You would do this in a similar way to working out total payroll percentage of the total salon net turnover, but this time focusing on individual performance. This will help the decision-making process regarding the employee and monitor the income they generate versus the cost of their salary, to ensure they are as profitable as possible.

Example

For instance, Joe takes home £1600 one month, which costs you £2000 to pay, inclusive of all your HMRC liabilities. He generates £4500.00 net turnover over the five-week pay period. He therefore costs you 44% in that pay period. If he had a vacation in that pay period, the cost would increase, as his turnover would be lower and he may well not earn much less. Bearing in mind the target percentage payroll for the entire salon, these figures show you which of your team members are the most profitable.

AN EMPLOYEE'S VIEW OF THE FINANCES

Continuing the example above, Joe may think that by bringing in an average of £4500 per month, which works out to be £5400 per month gross, he is turning over £1080 through the till per week and only taking home £320 per week, so that he makes the company a huge profit. He may not realise that you have to deduct VAT from his takings and add on the HMRC payments and liabilities to his salary, and therefore the profit margin will be vastly reduced. Add to that the cost of stock, heat and light, rent, rates, EPOS charges on their turnover and the unproductive support staff (receptionists, juniors, and so on) that are required to generate the turnover in the first place, and it is easy to see why a 10% pre-tax net profit aim is very realistic. It is a good idea to share the financial information so that employees do not have unrealistic views about the salon's profitability.

THE COLUMN AS A BUSINESS

The real aim of monitoring all this information is to attempt to develop an ethos among the team of:

- **empowerment** – they can impact on their performance because they have up-to-date information
- **autonomy** – they can make impact without assistance; it is under their control
- **financial success** – the more they perform, the better off they will be financially
- **responsibility** – they must take responsibility for their column as a business
- **ownership of performance** – as a manager you can guide, mentor and motivate them, but the KPIs on which they will be assessed are under their jurisdiction.

The fundamental principle is for the operator to see their column and clientele as a business within yours. If the right salary structure is set up, the sky is the limit for earnings, so tracking and benchmarking what you expect means that the ownership problem of poor performance is taken away from you and placed precisely where it should be – with the operator. As a salon owner or manager, you can provide people with the facilities and tools to perform, but the actual performance is down to them. It is, therefore, important to be clear and transparent about what you are looking for.

POOR PERFORMANCE SIGNS

The more experienced you get, the easier it will become to interpret the results of the KPIs on an individual basis. Here is my guide of what to look for.

Not hitting target

Are prices too high? Are they marketed at the correct tier/tariff? If yes, how are other operators in the tier performing? If they are doing well it is an individual problem, not a salon one. Look at the other KPIs for more clues.

Not hitting retail target

This really denotes a below average consultation and points to a poor analysis and diagnosis. Following the 'don't sell – advise' approach, if retail sales are non-existent there are areas of the consultation that are being missed.

Low percentage request

This is perhaps the most worrying. Why are people not booking back in? Something about the operator is causing a negative user experience. Use mystery clients to find out what it is. Perhaps the price does not match the experience.

Low occupancy rate

This must be looked at in conjunction with percentage request. If both are below par, there could be serious issues to address. Time is not being optimised, so link-selling and up-selling may be weak.

High percentage request

If this is too high, it can denote that no new clients are visiting the operator. If reception is choosing not to book them, what is the issue? An operator can have a fantastic percentage request, remember, even if they are only doing five clients a week – if all five have requested them, the figures can look misleadingly good.

Low average bill

This shows that the operator is not up-selling and link-selling their bookings or maximising their client spend. This is dangerous as it again points to weak consultation skills.

CONSULTATION AND RETAIL SKILLS

An operator's consultation and retail skills are vital and remain key to delivering the best performance possible. They should be the basis of our ongoing training and development plans.

PEOPLE PROBLEMS

Sometimes, you'll have to deal with team problems, and as their performance is crucial to your business, and this is a labour-intensive industry, the problems that your teams may have should be monitored to ensure they are happy and able to perform at optimum whilst at work and that the issue in question isn't having a detrimental effect on your business.

Different types of problems

Some team members might be unreliable; others can have problems in their private lives; some may have mental health problems, and others may not be performing for a plethora of other reasons. For example, some may be involved in criminal activity, others may be abusing substances and some may have poor health that is affecting their performance.

Other problems I have dealt with include: 'moonlighting', poaching clients, opening a salon nearby, theft of company property, breaches of company rules and regulations, personal hygiene problems, persistent sickness ('sickies'), religious issues, over-familiarity, breach of post-employment obligations and breach of the Data Protection Act.

All of the above can create many challenges, and some may require disciplinary procedure. However, it is important to deal with these issues as our job is to manage the gap between what the employee is delivering and what is expected of them and our duty is to help them get there if at all possible.

Employing staff over many years will see them experience good times and bad, so be prepared to deal with a multitude of different problems and try to develop a relationship that shows empathy and understanding through the difficult periods.

SUMMARY

Once again, consistency is key. The more consistent you are in asking for good performance, the more likely your teams are to deliver it. Communicating financial performance can be strangely opposed in our industry, with some salon managers I have known insisting that they inform their teams only on a 'need-to-know' basis. However, this is not advisable as it only encourages an attitude of secrecy and a lack of transparency.

We are in the business of providing a great salon environment and must put the structures in place to deliver a great client experience, with great branding, good products, excellent services and a good, sound technical team. All of that costs money. You make your profit from making this brand investment, marketing and positioning pay by ensuring that the operators you are relying upon to deliver the service play their part and get the customer back again. To do that, it is useful to track certain criteria and ensure they are reaching it. You need not apologise for this – you are in business, whether in this sector or not, to make money, and you should be encouraging your team to develop the same attitude to their own performance.

CHAPTER 8
SALARY PACKAGES

This chapter will look at the options for structuring your team salaries, from your trainees to your most senior operators. It will cover the different types of packages that you can offer, from basic deals to performance-related pay, and look at the pros and cons of each. We will look at other forms of pay and income, such as tips and bonuses, and also how self-employed contractors can operate in your business. The main aim of this chapter is to show you how you can calculate the salary packages that will work best for your salon.

SALARY STRUCTURES

Pay structures are vital to creating the right work ethic among your teams. Creating the right salary structures that motivate and incentivise staff to perform well is essential. Although you need to keep control of the payroll, as it is the single most significant cost to our business, it is also necessary to be generous with salaries in order to encourage good performance and, more significantly, to retain staff. This is why performance-related pay is common in our sector.

TYPES OF SALARY PACKAGES

There are several types of packages that could be set up for your team. Much will depend on their role as to which type of salary package may be applicable:

- **flat rate** (nonproductive staff such as receptionists, managers, etc)
- **flat rate plus commission** (junior team members or graduate productive staff may be on basic salaries but may also get commission on net retail sales)
- **flat rate or commission – whichever is the greater** (senior productive staff, such as therapists, stylists, technicians and manicurists).

Some salon managers and owners choose to pay their senior productive operators with a flat rate plus commission structure, instead of an either/or deal. This normally is a gross basic wage plus around 10% of their net takings (less VAT).

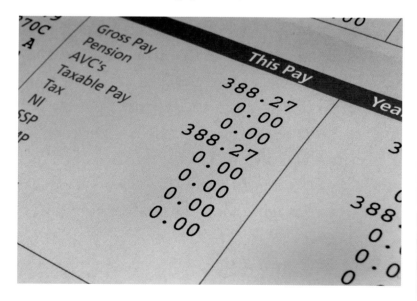

COMMISSION-RELATED PAY

Some commission structures contain caveats such as commission being scaled depending on turnover, or applicable only after a multiple of basic salary has been reached. From experience, I would say that commission needs to be kept as simple as possible in order for it to work well. The operator should not find working out their commission earned complicated; they should be able to work it out for themselves.

PAYING COMMISSION WHILE STAFF ARE ON HOLIDAY

Remember, while employees are taking paid holiday entitlement we are legally obliged (under the Working Time Directive) to pay them at the rate of their average earnings of the preceding 12 weeks, and not just basic salary; for staff on commission-related deals, this is an extra expense to bear in mind.

There is a principal in business that I use a lot; if you can't explain it to a 7 year old, it's too complicated! Similarly with commission, our teams need to be able to understand it easily for it to work well, so if it takes too much explanation, and confuses you, perhaps it's time to simplify it down.

DEALS FOR TRAINEES

It is worth, in accordance with the National Minimum Wage, setting different levels for first- to third-year trainees, so their pay increases on the anniversary of their joining the company. Rates will vary geographically. Whatever their level, also pay a commission on retail sales (net of VAT) so that they are incentivised from the start to embrace the 'don't sell – advise' approach and top up their earnings; 10% of net sales is standard.

Rates will vary geographically on what pay levels are acceptable, for instance London weighting.

DEALS FOR GRADUATE-LEVEL OPERATORS

Once team members are qualified and start life on the salon floor working on clients, they begin to go up the ladder rungs of both prices charged and commission rates paid. If starting on the either/or deal, the graduate-level operator might earn as follows:

- 35% of their net weekly takings (ie less VAT)
- or their gross basic wage, whichever is the greater
- **plus** 10% of their net retail sales (ie less VAT).

For example:

£200 gross basic or 35% of £1000 gross takings (=£833.33 net of VAT)

35% of £833.33 = £291.66 which is greater than £200 so £291.66 is their gross earning for that week, plus a commission of 10% of their net retail sales

This works well as their pay is not averaged out over the month, so if they have a good week they will benefit and if they have a bad week they will earn their basic. The goal is, of course, that they never earn their basic! They can easily work out their earnings simply by looking at the performance league and doing basic sums (especially if you show gross takings and net-of-VAT figures).

If it is not calculated weekly like this, they may have problems working it out for themselves. It may also lead to employees becoming demotivated if they do not perform well. If pay is averaged over the month, and the first two weeks are bad, the operator may be less likely to try hard for the remaining two weeks if they already feel there is not much point.

DEALS FOR MID-LEVEL OPERATORS

As the operator rises through each price tier, the commission percentage does not increase by much because their salary will increase as they are able to charge higher prices. Therefore, for the next level, commission might increase from 30% to 35%, or from 35 % to 37% or 38%. Much will depend on your location and what local pay rates tend to be as to what your starting commission rate will be. The same calculations will apply, but on the different percentage rates.

DEALS FOR SENIOR OPERATORS

Once operators reach a senior level, their rate of commission will increase again to anything from 35% to 40%. This will be calculated in exactly the same manner as before.

SPECIAL CIRCUMSTANCES

For those delivering exceptional performance, the most you can really pay is 45–48% of their net takings (plus their retail commission, which you may decide to increase to 15% of net sales). At this level of pay, the employee is not as profitable for the salon, but if their turnover is substantial, it is worth being generous in order to retain them. Even in a supersize salon, there may be only one or two people on a deal of this nature. They may be employees who have won awards or attracted celebrity clients and who will therefore be very valuable for building the reputation of your salon. Remember, employees of this stature may generate extra income through auxiliary sales and services for other team members or departments, so build that in when assessing their value.

COMMISSION-BASED PAY AND KPIs

The goal of this type of pay is to set a clear and transparent structure, where the team know that if they hit the KPIs and benchmarks, they will be rewarded financially – both via a rise in their commission rate and an increase in prices charged. But remember, percentage commission rates don't change once they have reached a tier – the levels remain the same. However, when the salon has a price increase across the board and when their tariff increases, they get an instant pay rise on both occasions, which helps them buy into the philosophy of delivering a great experience and charging accordingly. And, if the operator hits criteria and rises to a new level or rate and their pricing rises accordingly, they will get both an increase in their rate by going up a level and their tariff (prices charged).

PROS AND CONS OF COMMISSION-RELATED PAY

Pros

There are some points to consider in favour of commission-related pay. For example, that:

- it encourages a healthy attitude to financial success
- it motivates to optimise productivity
- it helps to retain staff as it is the closest thing to working for themselves
- price increases equal an instant salary increase too.

Cons

There are also some points to consider against commission-related pay. For example, that:

- when calculating holiday pay, averaging out the preceding 12 weeks' earnings can be expensive as commission must be included in these calculations
- it can be expensive and incurs tax and NIC liabilities.

PERFORMANCE-RELATED PAY

Some managers may be on basic salaries but can be incentivised on the salon's overall performance by receiving a performance-related bonus, payable on either a specific aspect of the salon's success or its overall figures and turnover. If a salon manager can directly affect the salon's financial performance, they could negotiate a bonus of, for example, a percentage of the increase in profitability they have managed to initiate.

TIPS AND GRATUITIES

While we all consider tips to be a fundamental perk of the operator's job, it is worth noting that tips and gratuities should be declared as taxable income. The law is different depending on who the tips are given to and who decides how they are shared out.

Tax implications

Cash tips given directly to the employee by the customer, without involving the employer, are subject to tax but not National Insurance. The operator is responsible for telling HMRC about these tips, and they should be shown and declared on the self-assessment tax return (if applicable). The operator should keep a record of all tips received so this can be done. For people who do not fill in a tax return, HMRC will estimate the tips the operator is likely to get and give them a tax code that will collect the tax through PAYE.

Tips that are added to a payment made by credit card are made to the employer and they may be pooled or passed on directly to the operator. If they are passed on directly, the employer is responsible for collecting tax on them through PAYE. If the employer decides how the tips are shared out, NICs are due and it is always the employer's responsibility to collect these through PAYE. If the employer does not decide or influence how the money is shared out among the employees, NICs will not be due. Pooled (or tronced) tips are gratuities that are shared out among staff. Whoever shares out the tips (the troncmaster), has to be notified to HMRC and as such is responsible for collecting income tax through PAYE; but if the employer decides (directly or indirectly) who this is, they are liable to pay NICs on the money, also.

(Source: www.hmrc.gov.uk)

If the salon owner or manager takes tips given by customers and does not pass them on to the employee, this can be considered illegal and can be deemed as theft. Employers cannot take payments made by customers to individuals in good faith as a contribution toward their salon running costs.

A tip is deemed to be a payment that is freely given by a customer, normally in return for a service, and is different from a compulsory service charge.

Refer to Book 1 Chapter 3 for more detail on NICs (National Insurance Contributions).

BONUSES

It may be wise to consider an annual performance-related or seasonal bonus for supervisors, department heads or trainers. It need not be hugely generous, but a financial thank you goes a long way for team members who are taking on extra responsibilities or to whom you delegate managerial tasks.

SELF-EMPLOYED CONTRACTORS

In our sector, there is much debate about having self-employed contractors working in a salon or renting a chair to an operator. There have been several legal test cases where salon owners have been reprimanded and have had to pay liabilities plus interest to HMRC because self-employed hairdressers, technicians or therapists have been deemed to be considered employed, and therefore VAT, NICs and so on, had to be backdated and paid.

If you have self-employed contractors in your salon, they must be deemed to be properly self-employed and cannot be under your control, direction or supervision. You should never choose to self-employ team members in order to escape HMRC liabilities. If any people within your salon are properly self-employed you must not treat them like other employees and should not, therefore, have any control over their working hours, days off or time away from the salon.

SELF EMPLOYED CONTRACTORS AGREEMENT

There must be a self-employed contractor's agreement between the individual and the salon which clearly points out, as a minimum:

- what the self-employed contractor is expected to pay as 'chair/room rental' (usually a percentage of their takings, for example 50%)
- what the rental consists of:
  - stock (possibly of their brand choice)
  - light, heat and water
  - use of a section/room/area
  - junior assistance, if applicable
  - reception usage (to book appointments and take bills)
  - public liability insurance (if appropriate – check with your insurance provider)
  - use of the salon's other services (refuse, etc)
- how VAT and other taxes are worked out in regard to the percentage rent, and whose liability they are; or if a flat rent, what it is and how often it is renewed
- how payments are going to be recorded, calculated and how often they will be made
- how invoicing for these payments will work
- how clients are determined as belonging to or originating from the salon or the self-employed contractor, ideally listing who belongs to whom, and ongoing, how this will be assessed
- that the salon is not responsible for furnishing them with new clients
- how prices are going to be charged, reviewed and increased and whether this is in accordance with the company's pricing policy
- notice period (from both sides) and post-contractual obligations.

Ideally, for HMRC to properly deem the operator as being self-employed, it would like to see a total independence from the salon, ie for the individual to have their own till, price list, receptionist and junior and act as an independent operator from other salon employees. Of course, this will not happen in the vast majority of salons, so the agreement that is in place needs to be watertight. Most importantly, the working relationship must *not* be one of employer/employee in order to be considered as viable self-employment. If this is not the case, the operator may well be considered to be employed and outstanding liabilities, including backdated taxes, could be applicable.

PROS AND CONS OF SELF-EMPLOYMENT

There are some arguments for and against self employment.

For

An argument for self-employment is that it means less expense to the employer – no paid vacation, no NICs, etc.

Against

There are more arguments against self-employment from the employer's point of view:

- no control over working hours, periods of absence, days worked, and possibly appointment times and prices
- cannot ask them to comply with staff rules and regulations
- cannot control, direct or supervise them, nor discipline them
- cannot benchmark them using KPIs, nor appraise or review their performance
- cannot instil a company ethos or way of working
- furnishing them with new clients needs careful thought, and agreement must be in place about how this is handled (for the operator this may not be motivating for their long-term progression in building up a strong clientele)
- the contractor is responsible for their own accounting, invoicing and tax liabilities which can be a little too complicated for them to administer correctly (helping them in such matters further echoes more of an employment relationship so is not deemed appropriate).

PAYING YOUR TEAM

You can pay staff on a weekly or monthly basis and by cheque or direct transfer into their bank account. If you choose monthly, it can either be by calendar date or by a four- or five-week pay period (whichever is applicable). Staff tend to prefer the latter option, as they can calculate their potential earnings more easily if it coincides with the week-end periods. Whatever method you choose (I prefer monthly, but calculated weekly so that staff can understand more easily), you will need to provide staff with a pay slip that shows the following information:

- the gross wage
- the amount of any fixed deductions and what they are for (stakeholder pensions, etc)
- the amount of any variable deductions and what they are for (PAYE, NICs, etc)
- the net wage.

Payroll can be complicated and if your managerial time is at a premium, it is worth using a clerk or your accountant to administer your payroll for you.

REGULARLY REVIEW

It is never worth losing a good member of staff over a small salary increase. Always calculate the cost of the raise against the potential costs of replacement, the possible loss of incremental and auxiliary business, the time cost involved in recruiting and interviewing, as well as the cost of advertising the position. It is also prudent to offer pay increases before being asked. Analyse employees during the appraisal system and make sure that you are aware of who needs to be given a commission rise or move up a level – it feels much sweeter for the employee not to have to ask for it!

SUMMARY

No salon ever wins a prize for having the lowest payroll. It is all about creating the right balance between the productive salaries (and ensuring these are kept inline with regular individual reviews of pay as a percentage of turnover) and nonproductive team members whose salaries need to be paid out of the turnover generated by the productive team.

Keeping a commission structure simple and uncomplicated so that team members can calculate their performance for themselves is vital; do not create a system that requires too much explanation – the key really is keeping it simple.

If you do wish to go down the self-employed route, think long and hard about the implications. Make sure your agreement is watertight (take legal advice) and ensure that both you and the individual fully understand their liabilities.

CHAPTER 9
APPRAISALS

This chapter will cover a vital element of your role – conducting appraisals. We will look at how often they should be instigated, how long they should last, when and where to carry them out and what to cover. We will also look at what you need to be monitoring and comparing against (KPIs) and how to deal with the forms and procedures for compiling the information. Most importantly, we will focus on how to handle appraisals and achieve the goal of leaving the employee motivated and focused on the plans for the future.

WHAT IS AN APPRAISAL?

Appraising team members is a crucial part of the salon manager's role. One-to-one reviews with your team are a great opportunity for you to encourage staff development and, most importantly, they are a time for the employee to 'be heard' and to voice their concerns and opinions.

Appraisals are not, however, a chance for the employee to berate the company or remonstrate over collective feelings. Appraisal language should be 'me' and 'I' not 'we'. Keep the equilibrium right; you need to create the right balance between constructive feedback and salon politics. The appraisal process should be a two-way discussion. If held in the right way, with the manager in control but willing to listen to comments, they can be equally productive for both parties.

HOW IT WORKS

An appraisal should be 80% listening and 20% speaking on the manager's part. Listening is only truly effective if we practise active listening and are fully engaged with the employee. An employee who is looking forward to their appraisal dreads nothing more than a manager who is not giving them the attention they deserve. You must not be distracted – it is vital to give the team member your undivided attention. Ask open questions and look for clues in the answers. Ask joint questions that engage the employee – such as 'what do you think will help us to achieve better results in this area?' and mirror body language to show empathy and encourage a connection between you, allowing the employee to speak without interruption.

HOW TO HOLD AN APPRAISAL

HOW OFTEN?

Ideally, an appraisal should be held at least every 12 months, and at most every six months. If they are done more often than this they lose weight and gravitas. An appraisal is not a quick performance-review-style chat – it should be a serious look at an employee's career development, performance and plans for the future; so hold them less often but make them more important. Conduct all your appraisals at one time rather than spreading them throughout the year. For instance, my appraisals are divided into two sections – with senior staff appraisals being held every January and those for junior team members every August – which enables me to compile my information and use it for the appraisal process. In sticking to this system the employee knows what to expect and when. It works well to create a feeling of 'it's our appraisal time' so issues are brought to the fore and dealt with.

HOW LONG?

To do an appraisal properly will take about an hour of uninterrupted time. Hold the appraisal out of the salon environment – go to a local coffee bar or hotel foyer – somewhere where you will not be interrupted. Switch off your mobile phone. Give the employee your undivided attention. Schedule it with at least two weeks' notice, informing each employee when and where it will take place. You should not do it at the last minute without any prior warning; give your employees time to prepare.

MONITORING TOOLS

There are some different tools you can use to help you prepare for the appraisal procedure. However, before you conduct each appraisal, you should first read back through the employee's previous appraisal form (which should be with you during the process) to look at the previously agreed action plan and review its implementation. It is also a good idea to review individual self-assessment forms and highlight the areas for development and training that the employee has uncovered.

Attendance sheets

Attendance sheets are like your salon register; you can use them to record and track your team's attendance and they enable you to see a whole year at a glance. They should be kept in a file (with past years' sheets filed for reference) and completed every day. Record your information using the following system (or create one of your own!):

X = day off
/ = present
T = training
LD = Lieu day
V = vacation
U/P = unpaid leave
L/20 = late 20 minutes
S = sick
U/A = unauthorised absence

Attendance sheets are a great tool to use to track staff's comings and goings, and are essential for logging down holidays and planning your staff vacation rota too. They are particularly effective during the appraisal procedure because they enable you to be specific about matters such as punctuality and attendance.

RICHARD WARD HAIR & METROSPA
ATTENDANCE SHEET FOR '11 TO '12

Name: SALLY
Job Title: STYLIST
Normal Day Off: MONDAY
Employed/SelfEmp: EMP

LIEU DAYS
1 E.MAY
1 L.MAY

Week Commencing		M	T	W	T	F	S	N.B
April	4	X	/	/	/	/	/	
	11	X	/	/	/	/	/	
	18	X	/	/	/	X	/	
	25	X	/	/	/	X	/	
May	2	X	/	/	/	/	/	
	9	X	/	S	/	/	/	
	16	X	/	/	/	/	/	
	23	X	V	V	V	V	V	
	30	X						
June	6	X	/	/	/	/	/	
	13	X	/	/	/	/	/	
	20	X	V	V	/	/	/	
	27	X	/	/	/	/	/	
July	4	X	S	S	/	/	/	
	11	X	/	/	/	/	/	
	18	X	/	/	/	/	/	
	25	X	/	/	/	/	/	
August	1							
	8							
	15							
	22							
	29	X						
Sept	5	X	V	V	V	V	V	
	12							
	19							
	26							

Week Commencing		M	T	W	T	F	S	N.B
October	3							
	10							
	17							
	24							
	31							
November	7							
	14							
	21							
	28							
December	5							
	12							
	19							
	26	X	X					
January	2	X						
	9							
	16							
	23							
	30							
February	6							
	13							
	20							
	27							
March	5							
	12							
	19							
	26							

Paid Holiday Entitlement:
(i.e. number of days earned since April) 20

NO OF DAYS HOLIDAY LEFT
13 8

USING FIGURES

Average weekly takings

There are some criteria and formulae you can use to calculate the average weekly takings. These can take into account any time out of the salon, for instance holidays, and look at the actual average over the productive time worked.

Use this formula:

Average weekly takings $= x \div y$

$x =$ total net takings

$y =$ number of days actually worked in the period of time divided by number of days normally worked per week

So, if an employee's total net takings were £7000 over the course of 3 months (13 weeks), and they had taken one week's holiday, you would work the average weekly takings out as follows:

$x = £7000$

$y = 60$ days worked $\div 5$ days normally worked per week $= 12$

$x \div y$ (7000 $\div$ 12) $= £583.34$ average weekly takings

6-monthly figures

However often you decide to calculate them, it is a good idea to publish, periodically (and ideally to coincide with appraisals) three- or six-monthly figures. Much like a performance league, these figures should form the basis of the reviewing procedure, but you can choose – between structured performance reviews – to let staff know more information and show a league of the top money takers and performers. These leagues give operators a real insight into their salon average and also enable them to compete psychologically with their peers and aim for better performance.

THE APPRAISAL FORM

The layout and content of the form is as crucial as its implementation. Make sure you cover the KPIs, but remember that any price increases that have been instigated will affect these figures. Look at:

- actual average weekly takings against target and compared with last appraisal figure
- actual average weekly retail sales against target and compared to last appraisal figure
- average bill against last appraisal figure
- percentage request against last appraisal figure
- percentage occupancy rate against last appraisal figure
- technical referrals or other referrals, if applicable.

Ask for feedback on each of the areas listed above, or whatever you want to monitor for your salon. Then ask some general questions for feedback, such as how the employee feels about their link-selling, up-selling, appearance, attendance, punctuality, motivation, team work, standard of technical work (theirs), and other less specific areas such as: training, education, salon prices, services, treatments and innovations.

Leave a large comment box for them to note down any other issues they may want to raise with you, too, as well as leaving plenty of space to write your own comments and also room to note down any action that is required.

Stylist appraisal form

HW to fill in

Name:	
Position/tier:	
Length of service:	

Date:	
For period from/to:	

Occupancy rate:	
Previous occupancy rate:	

Average gross weekly take:	
Last appraisal weekly take:	

	(% +/-)	New target
Target		
Target		

Average weekly technical:	
Last appraisal weekly technical:	

		New target
Target		
Target		

	CH	Total
Average weekly retail:		
Last appraisal weekly retail:		

		New target
Target		
Target		

Average bill:	
% Request rate:	

Last App		
Last App		

Your comments on your financial performance (above):

HW comments on above:

Stylist appraisal form
You to fill in
Self Assessment (Please tick)

	Excellent	Very good	Good	Fair	Needs work	Poor
Appearance						
Attendance						
Punctuality						
Teamwork						
Motivation						
Attitude						
Column timekeeping						
Occupancy rate						
Average weekly takings						
Technical referrals						
Retail sales						
Average bill						
Client retention – request rate						
Customer service						
Link selling						
Standard of work						

Self assessment comments:

Manager to fill in
Managers name: **Manager's assessment (Please tick)**

	Excellent	Very good	Good	Fair	Needs work	Poor
Appearance						
Attendance						
Punctuality						
Teamwork						
Motivation						
Attitude						
Column timekeeping						
Occupancy rate						
Average weekly takings						
Technical referrals						
Retail sales						
Average bill						
Client retention – request rate						
Customer service						
Link selling						
Standard of work						

Gavins comments:

Stylist appraisal form

Gavins comments:

Department heads comments:

Stylist appraisal form

Achievement of ten steps – Gavin's assessment

	Excellent	Very good	Good	Fair	Needs work	Poor
1. Greet personally						
2. Tour and recommend colleagues						
3. Inform client of reward points						
4. Email cards						
5. Indepth consultation						
6. Indepth analysis of scalp & hair						
7. Surpass client expectations						
8. Escorting client to reception						
9. Re-book/treatment plan						
10. Showing products/advice						

You to fill in

Achievement of ten steps – Self Assessment

	Excellent	Very good	Good	Fair	Needs work	Poor
1. Greet personally						
2. Tour and recommend colleagues						
3. Inform client of reward points						
4. Email cards						
5. Indepth consultation						
6. Indepth analysis of scalp & hair						
7. Surpass client expectations						
8. Escorting client to reception						
9. Re-book/treatment plan						
10. Showing products/advice						

Action points: (GH or RW to complete)

THE APPRAISAL PROCEDURE

You should give the form containing only the statistical information to the employee a good week or two before the date of the appraisal, and encourage them to prepare. Do not add any of your comments at this stage; let the numbers speak for themselves. Make sure the employee understands the figures and KPIs that you are going to be discussing, allowing them plenty of time to ask any questions about them in advance of the appraisal. By asking the employee to comment on the figures, you are keeping the review format quite structured and focused only on them and their performance.

It is worth creating a different appraisal form for each sector so you can refine it to include more specific, relevant information. Think about having one for stylists/technicians, and creating a different version for therapists, receptionists and juniors and adapting its content to suit.

USING THE APPRAISAL FORM

Ask the employee to return the form a few days before the appraisal, and compile any other information you may need, such as feedback from other sources. This also enables you to have a brief look at the employee's comments before the appraisal start to give you the 'heads up' on what they are feeling about their performance.

At the actual appraisal, go through the form step by step. Start by asking them in general how they are feeling about things, then move on to the statistics and read out their response to the KPIs one by one, discussing each comment and sharing your feedback. Communicate your viewpoint on their comments at each stage and share input from any relevant supervisors or managers whom you have asked to comment. Where action needs to be taken, once each area has been discussed in depth, agree the action and when and how it will be implemented.

DEVELOPMENT PLAN

Creating a development plan is key. You will only find out what makes your employee tick by asking them critical questions – where do they want to be in six months' time? How can you help them to get there? A good appraisal is when the team member is asking for your input and feedback into how they could improve and reach their next salon goal (having already identified the information for themselves), so steer the appraisal in this direction by asking leading questions.

Spare some time for personal chat about what is going on in their lives (perhaps buying a property, getting married, and so on) and general comments. It is a great way to find out what motivates your staff – it is not always financial, although it does tend to be! Career progression may be more motivating to some people than earnings. Take note of any goals and aspirations they have or areas they want to develop personally. Make sure there are no other issues that they want to bring up before the appraisal comes to an end.

THE 'ATES

I always use the '-ate' words for any kind of people management, and never more so than during the appraisal process:
- communicate
- educate
- motivate
- delegate.

It is important to:
- communicate to our teams on their performance
- educate them on what we expect
- motivate them to perform
- delegate the responsibility for the performance to them.

PRAISE-CRITICISE-PRAISE

I find the 'praise – criticise – praise' approach works best. Point out what the employee is doing well first then lead on to what they could do better and finally finish on a positive note – as this tends to deliver the best results. Focusing only on the negative and forgetting to thank and verbally reward any good performance is highly demotivating for staff.

POOR PERFORMANCE SIGNS

We have already discussed where problems might be arising; perhaps more importantly, we need to look at what to do about the issues. Ideally, the employee will have already spotted any problem areas for themselves when filling out their appraisal form; if they have not, probe to see that they have noticed and point out the areas you are concerned about. In bringing the problem areas to their attention, show them how other operators in their tier or price level are performing (not to antagonise, more to point out that other people are able to meet requirements, so it's an individual problem and not a salon one).

First, you should give the employee the chance to give his or her view of the problem. Why do they think they are not performing? What do they think they need to do about it? How can you help them? The following problems may arise.

Not hitting target

Start by looking back at previous performance. Is it a new problem? Is it a gradual decline? If prices have increased since the last performance review figures, and takings are dropping, then what percentage are they down in real terms? If prices are constant and figures are still in decline, look at other operators in the relevant price tier and see if there are trends. If not, look at the remaining KPIs to get your answer. It will most certainly be there somewhere.

Not hitting retail target

If this is a problem, revisit and role-play the client consultation. Assess how well diagnosis and analysis is being carried out. Develop a checklist of key consultation points to sharpen up analysing and prescribing skills. Use role play and retrain, as well as conducting retraining on product knowledge. Book a time to review and revisit figures, say in three months' time.

Low percentage request

This issue should be the most concerning. Analyse across other team members in the price tier and work out how far the performance is out. Remind the employee of the benchmark figure and ask them to assess what they think may be lacking in their visit experience which is resulting in the poor performance. It may be wise to have a mystery shopper report completed before the appraisal so you can feed back on areas for improvement. Stress how vital it is that seven out of 10 customers will want to rebook, and remind them of the importance of hitting this KPI for their future development.

Low occupancy rate

If the employee's rate of productivity is below par, it may be directly related to their ability to link-sell and cross-refer. Up-selling is also vital, to ensure they maximise their time. Take some examples of their appointment column over the previous few weeks and show them ways in which their time could have been made more productive.

High percentage request

This may show a lack of new clients and, if there is no regular replenishment, it could indicate stagnation in performance. Find out why they feel they are not being recommended and encourage a cross-referral buddy system with colleagues who work in a similar way to stimulate the flow of transient or new business. The ideal percentage request is between 85–90%, but over 70% is acceptable. Any lower and it's concerning, any higher and it may indicate a lack of recommendation, another possible concern.

Low average bill

If this is lower than for other colleagues in the same price tier, this can signal that the employee is not up-selling their time productively or encouraging a multiservice approach with their clientele.

WHAT TO DO NEXT

If there are any serious concerns that may later lead to disciplinary action, they should be flagged up before the appraisal, but if they are not, it is vital to flag them up during the appraisal; failure to do so on your part could cause problems later.

Once an area that requires action is jointly agreed by you and the employee, you both need to agree an action plan to remedy the problem. Through plenty of probing and open questions, you should be able to establish what requires action. Make a note of any action points and confirm when and how the plan will be implemented, gaining agreement from the employee that they concur with the plan and that time frames for improvement are reasonable.

DOS AND DON'TS OF CONDUCTING AN APPRAISAL

There are some useful points to consider when conducting an appraisal.

Things to do include the following.

Do:

- agree a plan of action and stick to it, reviewing when agreed
- listen well – remember that you may be doing 10 appraisals, but the employee only cares about his or hers

- have staff files, attendance sheets, previous appraisal forms, figures and statistics with you and on hand; do not be vague
- stay in control – remember, *you* are reviewing *their* performance
- confront any difficult issues and raise concerns
- get feedback from others – supervisors, department heads, trainers and deputy managers can all provide invaluable information and give you deeper insight into any performance-related issues.

There are also some things that you should not do.

Don't:
- get personal – keep the emotion out of the appraisal and stay focused on the issues
- let the appraisal become the employee berating the company or telling you what you are doing wrong
- apologise for wanting good performance in the first place, nor apologise for the employee's poor performance – it is not your problem, it is theirs (and the fact that other operators are achieving their targets demonstrates this for you)
- forget to do your homework – have information to hand to back you up
- be too informal – an appraisal is a serious procedure
- allow yourself to be interrupted – there should not be any possibility of you being disturbed
- allow the employee to talk in terms of 'we'; remind them that this is their individual performance review and not a review of other team members (staff often do this as it makes them feel they are not alone, but it's infuriating for the manager!).

SUMMARY

Conducting appraisals is an essential element of your role as manager or owner, as well as being vital for the continued development of your teams. Allow time to run your appraisal system properly and ensure you have up-to-date information to deliver to your teams.

Tailor-make your appraisal form so it fits your salon's KPIs and keeps focused on how the team are going to reach them. Make sure that staff are regularly aware of their performance via your weekly performance league as this makes your job easier. Remember, the goal is for the employee to discover it for themselves if they are not performing well in comparison with their peers.

CHAPTER 10
COMPETITIONS AND INCENTIVES

This chapter will explore other ways to encourage and motivate your team. We will look at the targeted incentives you can come up with to achieve specific results, and how to effectively run team competitions to increase sales and productivity. We will also look at the various types of programmes and promotional activities you can organise for your employees to deliver tangible results, and also how to communicate these, and other matters, to your team via staff meetings.

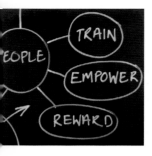

INCENTIVISING YOUR TEAM

Incentivising through pay is vital, but it is also important to conduct other performance-related programmes on an ongoing basis to achieve other essential KPIs. It can be healthy to run competitions from time to time, to stimulate the team and encourage them to achieve more. These can take the form of a biannual, quarterly or annual event, or they can be held sporadically to liven up team results and get instant increases in performance and productivity. You can also choose to focus them around products, for instance running them to coincide with new product launches or tying them in to brands that you use professionally in the salon.

COMPETITIONS

There are many ways of running team competitions and they can be centred around specific areas of performance, turnover or retail sales. Alternatively, you can make them more specific, for instance, using them to launch a new treatment or service and recommending bookings. If the competition is product-related, ask your manufacturer or supplier to help with prizes and promotional material to promote the incentive to the team. Make sure they are adequately trained before you start the competition; some refreshment or retraining may be required to get them fully up to speed and confident in their product knowledge, or some role play to revisit their retailing and consulting skills may be useful.

For maximum impact you should never run more than one competition at one time – keep the team focused on one element of their performance at a time. Ensure they are fully aware of:
- what the incentive involves
- how it will be tracked and monitored
- when it will start and finish
- what the prize is
- when the winner will be announced.

Keep all information about the competition posted on the staff noticeboard for the duration of the incentive's running time, and give regular daily or weekly updates so the team can track their own performance.

RETAIL COMPETITIONS

Competitions based on retail sales often work well. This is particularly the case in the run-up to a busy period like Christmas, when team members really have a chance to shine and retail purchases are a focus for their clients. Launch your competition with a staff meeting to get everybody excited and motivated and show them the prizes, if possible.

STRUCTURING A COMPETITION

You can track winners through:
- monetary value or takings, if applicable
- percentage increase on their specific target
- points per transaction/booking/sale.

It may be more productive to use a percentage increase system, as if you choose a monetary value and one particular team member steams ahead, the others could become demotivated and give up. Points work well too, as people tend to find it easier to compare themselves with other team members when using a 'universal' system of reward. There could be a prize winner every week, to keep people motivated, and an overall winner and runner-up.

Similarly, you can use a system where each day there is a small prize for the top performer, as many team members can benefit and achieve results. You can then run a major prize for the person who has won the most times, so everybody is in with a chance.

MAXIMISING COMPETITIONS

Do not run competitions for too long – staff become immune to them if they drag on. Keep them time-specific – four to six weeks is normally the optimum time to deliver the best results. Adopt a 'less is more' approach to running competitions and vary the content so the same team members are not always winning; for instance, you could alternate between retail competitions and those targeted on treatments or services.

INCENTIVES

Unlike a competition, which is time-specific, an incentive can be an ongoing reward programme to encourage specific areas of performance. You can incentivise your team on any element of their work, so ensure the incentive is targeted to benefit the salon and encourage weaker areas of performance that have already been identified. You can also run incentives based on cross-referrals and recommendations from team members and between departments.

Think about incentivising on the following areas which will greatly influence the individual's performance: up-selling and link-selling.

UP-SELLING

This involves upgrading an appointment into a bigger service; so, for example, an appointment for a leg wax becomes a leg wax and bikini wax, or a blow-dry becomes cut and blow-dry. Up-selling automatically earns the up-seller increased turnover and therefore salary (if incentivised pay is in force).

LINK-SELLING

Link-selling involves cross-referring other treatments that naturally tie in; for example, a client having a pre-holiday self-tan booking is encouraged to have an anti-fade colour gloss. This may involve other departments and team members but encourages an ethos of cross-promotion.

Link-selling to other team members can be rewarded through other ways than increased turnover. For instance, this might include treatments delivered by the recipient team member in salon time in acknowledgement and appreciation for the recommendation, or even extra financial incentives to reward the referral.

IN-SALON AWARDS

Creating your own awards programme can be an excellent way of encouraging a salon ethos of continuity and progression within the company. Have an annual in-salon awards event to celebrate excellence, reward skills, honour technical ability, acknowledge performance, praise hard work and identify those with excellent attitudes, as well congratulating team members on their achievements. You can focus on:

- customer service achievements
- team members of the year (by department, if applicable)
- junior of the year (this is fun if voted for by the senior team members)
- artistic work/photographic work (if applicable)
- achievement of KPIs
- progression within the company
- personal development.

Whatever you decide to reward, make sure team members are fully aware of the criteria by which winners are judged so the event remains positive and does not conjure up any negative connotations.

Ask a representative from your chosen supplier to come and judge/present awards, and take plenty of photos for internal marketing and external PR (trade and consumer – it is worth asking a local journalist to judge in order to cement relationships and encourage coverage).

Hold your annual ceremony at the same time every year, for continuity.

TALENT SHOWCASING

Think about having an annual 'Apprentice of the Year' or 'Young Therapist of the Year' competition which, unlike the in-salon award 'Junior of the Year' (which is focused on salon performance and day-to-day work), enables the trainees and graduates to showcase their practical and creative skills to their peers, friends and family members and demonstrate their level of competence.

Give them a creative brief to produce some commercial work (such as they have regularly seen in the salon) which reflects their level of training – senior trainees may want to experiment and do some avant-garde work. Challenge them to come up with a mood board showing their inspiration and to present their fully-styled, total look model to their peers, detailing what they have done technically (cut, colour or finish for hair, or nails/make-up for beauty) and explaining why certain techniques were used. Ask them to base their look on forthcoming catwalk trends to demonstrate their ability to understand fashion's influence on hair, beauty and make-up.

Judging

Call in guest judges or get the senior team to score, taking their length of service into account. Depending on the number of entrants, you may decide to award a prize for each year/level or each specialist area.

It works well to get the parents involved by inviting them to events such as these, as it will help demonstrate where their loved one is in their training in comparison with their peers, and will also show how much thought and effort was put in on the apprentice's behalf. Offer refreshments to the trainee's guests and ensure you allow some time afterwards should any of them wish to raise any concerns with you.

LONG SERVICE AWARDS

Rewarding longevity of employment is a great way to encourage staff retention. Recognising and praising long service creates a great role model for younger team members who are aspiring to progress. You can choose to award five, ten, fifteen or twenty years' service either on a particular event evening or at a Christmas party or other team celebration, such as part of your annual awards. Make the award valuable by offering a trophy or engraved platter or other memento to make the event special. Photograph the evening and provide coverage of the event internally via your website (if applicable) or marketing material, or externally to local media.

REWARD POINTS

If retailing is proving challenging for your team, it is worth considering an incentive where staff are rewarded on their sales. For example, one point per £1 of retail products sold, which can only be redeemed once they reach certain levels, for instance 200 points, 500 points, 1000 points, etc. You can reward staff with vouchers for a dinner for two, musical, theatre or for their favourite retailer, for example. Programmes like this encourage loyalty and help to prolong service, and can also be used for promoting specific treatments and services periodically, as well; for example, double points for a certain period of time.

BIRTHDAY SCHEMES

There may be tax implications for any added incentives you give your team check with your accountant or at www.hmrc.gov.uk

It is a good idea to have a programme to celebrate either the staff member's individual birthdays or their anniversary of working for the company. You can run a programme where you reward each year of service (either on the employee's birthday or on their anniversary) by giving them vouchers or prizes to the value of a certain amount per year they have worked for you. This is a particularly good way of thanking staff for their loyalty and, again, encourages the long-service mentality.

STAFF MEETINGS

It is really important to hold whole-team meetings regularly, at least every six to eight weeks. You can also hold more specific meetings to cover more detailed information when necessary – for example, reception team, therapists and nail technicians only, technical team members, juniors and apprentices or styling team only. But a whole team get-together is vital on a regular basis to help cement their working relationships.

Meetings are great to discuss matters, pass on relevant information, brainstorm and generally inform and discuss plans so everybody knows what is going on. Staff like to be communicated to and to be kept up to date with any information. You can share good news, reward excellent performance, praise promoted team members and generally share any issues and information.

KEEPING A STAFF MEETING LOG

From time to time, urgent information will need to be communicated when it will not always be possible to hold a staff meeting. It is fine to put up memos in between the regular meetings, but always note them down in your 'staff meeting log'. This is a book that you can keep permanently to record information you need to share with your team at the next meeting, so that vital things do not get forgotten and you can verbally recap on interim information.

HOLDING A STAFF MEETING

Make sure you inform your team about staff meetings well in advance. If holding the meeting after working hours, you should provide some refreshments and give people the opportunity to arrange childcare and alter plans by giving them plenty of notice. If possible, prepare an agenda and put it on the staff noticeboard so they are aware of what you are going to be discussing, and after the meeting put up minutes of what was discussed so any non-attendees are aware of what was covered.

Always allow time for an open forum session to allow team members to raise any issues, but stay in control and keep it positive. Do not allow personal issues between team members to become the focus; if matters being discussed are not appropriate do not be afraid to suggest that people should stay behind to discuss the matter privately in more depth. Making sure issues are relevant to the whole team keeps the meeting focused and of interest to everyone.

DON'T WORRY IF YOU COVER THE SAME GROUND

From experience, you will undoubtedly find that you will repeat yourself regularly when holding staff meetings. I always say that I could turn my staff meetings record book to any page over the preceding 10 years and the agenda would be the same. Joking apart, rule enforcement is a major element of the salon manager's role, and you will find the same issues arise time and again. Do not despair – this is par for the course for many of us!

DOS AND DON'TS OF STAFF MEETINGS

There are some particular points to follow and also things not to do when holding staff meetings.

Things that you should do include the following.

Do:

- welcome new team members
- applaud any changes in role or promotions to a new level for any team members
- use the 'if the cap fits, wear it' analogy when mentioning sensitive issues, rather than referring to team members specifically; however, if it is an historical or repeated issue, feel free to 'name and shame', but in a light-hearted manner
- encourage feedback and run through any proposed ideas with the team for their input; make them part of the solution, not part of the problem; (empowering team members to come to conclusions and make decisions is vital for the salon's overall success).

There are also some things to avoid. Don't:

Don't:

- mention anything contentious if disciplinary action has commenced with the individual concerned regarding any matter you are raising
- let the meeting get too personal; stay in control of the open forum session
- linger too long on any issues that only apply to a minority of the team – save these for the relevant department meetings instead.

SUMMARY

Aside from financially incentivised salary structures, make sure you run regular competitions for your team members to keep them enthused and motivated. Keep them short and snappy for maximum impact.

Incentivising on other elements of performance may be longer term, so ensure you know what to monitor carefully and work out how you are going to feed back the results and rewards. Think about holding awards ceremonies internally and celebrating and recognising long service to encourage staff retention, as well as holding 'soirées' to showcase talent.

Whole-team staff meetings are crucial to the smooth running of the salon but, for more specific areas, have department meetings instead. Give people plenty of notice and ensure you run through the agenda later with any team members who were unable to attend. In between meetings, record any information that you do not want to omit from the next meeting's agenda.

CHAPTER 11
CAREER PATHING AND STAFF RETENTION

This chapter will cover the most important element of success: staff retention. We will look at how to assess your salon's staff turnover and how to find each team member's talents and aspirations then ensure you focus on helping them develop to their full potential through creating a career path for them to follow. We will look at developing a hierarchy of roles, creating a management structure and the day-to-day reporting lines required to get everyone delegating, happy and communicating well, so the salon is running as efficiently as possible.

A GOOD TEAM

The key to running a successful salon really is down to having a good team who stay with you. The more people stay and the longer they remain, the greater the following they will build and the more you can rely upon their loyal clienteles and their resulting business. If you have this solid foundation, maximising their profitability is merely the icing on the cake.

MINIMISING STAFF TURNOVER

Our industry need not be transient with staff coming and going – we have to look at what we may be doing wrong if team members fail to stay with us and staff turnover is high. People will always naturally move along, but your staff turnover – however you choose to calculate it – should be as minimal as possible.

Every senior team member or turnover-producing operator who leaves our salons leaves us, as managers and owners, exposed. Not only might they work in a rival salon, which naturally could mean clients could follow them, but they could open up a salon of their own. Moreover, unless you have stringent contractual arrangements, there could be nothing stopping them from advertising the fact that they have relocated or worse – taking confidential client information with them and contacting their clients to inform them of their whereabouts.

It does not end there – for every team member we lose, we run the risk of others following and then not only do we risk losing their clienteles, but there is also the loss of possible ancillary business. For instance, say a senior stylist leaves and most of their clients choose to follow them. It is not just the demise of their turnover we have to factor in, but the extra salon services their clients will also be spending on elsewhere – colour, manicure, retail sales, etc. The original impact of the loss can therefore be more significant than we at first thought.

STAFF PROGRESSION

It is, therefore, critical to our performance to ensure we have plans and goals for our teams to aspire to and to continually motivate them, so they feel they are making progression. In effect we are creating career paths for them to follow. We will never be able to satisfy someone's desire to have their own salon or to follow their dreams on a larger scale. However, by delegating some managerial responsibilities to those who want them, and sharing the problems of owning or managing a salon or spa with them, we minimise the risk of them pursuing their goal – especially if they see the role and its resulting responsibilities entailed without the 'rose tinted glasses' on.

Furthermore, by structuring our salaries so they are earning well and are feeling incentivised, we can do no more to keep them. Ultimately, people will always do what they choose to do, but structuring things correctly can minimise staff turnover.

Some staff may be happy to plod on – the plodders are as crucial to our overall success as the 'dynamos' who are ambitious and driven. Getting the right mix is vital, and making sure you take time to discover what makes all of your team tick on an individual basis is ever more important to making sure they stay loyal to your business. Remember, the 80/20 rule applies to our teams as much as it does our wardrobes (we wear 20% of our wardrobe 80% of the time) and we can all be guilty of spending 80% of our HR time on 20% of our team –the most demanding ones! Sometimes, the 'plodders' – the ones who are happy with their lot and not ambitious to develop further, other than regular training and good salaries – can get forgotten; they must not be, as you may find they form the bread and butter of your business, so keeping them happy is equally vital.

DISCOVERING TALENTS AND STRENGTHENING STRENGTHS

One of the most rewarding, empowering and fulfilling elements of the salon manager's role is to discover hidden potential and identify staff's strengths. There are few other sectors with so many spin-off careers and opportunities and, as more team members are realising, our enterprising sector offers a myriad of career opportunities and diverse paths.

Some team members will not naturally be able to identify their talents and often, even if they could, would not really know how to harness them and capitalise on them. One of the few advantages of our sector being unregulated is that people have the opportunity to change and develop their roles without the need for red tape and stringent qualification guidelines. This leaves us, as managers and owners, to spot and develop potential and guide it in the right direction and allow it to bloom and grow.

HOW TO DO IT

Identifying the hidden talents that people have is largely done through a good mix of:
- on-the-job assessment (during the course of their normal working duties)
- delegation of tasks
- careful and detailed assessment and appraisal.

Giving someone a different task outside their normal job remit can help to discover other strengths which may have remained unnoticed otherwise; but finding out what makes them tick is even more crucial for discovering those hidden talents that are waiting to be maximised.

HIDDEN TALENT LIES WHERE YOU LEAST EXPECT IT!

I once interviewed someone for the part-time job of salon cleaner and found, upon probing, that she really wanted the position to get close to her hidden passion: hairdressing. Being Portuguese, and not knowing the British system, she assumed she was too old in her late twenties to retrain for hairdressing. But her desire to work as a hairdresser was so strong that I encouraged her to undergo an apprenticeship with us. She is now one of the mainstays of our artistic team. Her ability to speak different languages means she can pursue other opportunities on behalf of the company overseas. This little story of that employee is perhaps what I am most proud of in the entire history of my managerial career.

WHAT MOTIVATES?

Finding out what makes people tick is vital. We are wrong to assume that everyone is ultimately motivated by money, although often financial recompense is firmly at the root of our motivation!

If you are not sure what motivates one of your team members, simply ask them to complete a chart which will help them to identify for themselves what makes them tick. The answers can be surprising and it is a great exercise to conduct regularly as our motivational drive is much dictated by our (ever changing) personal circumstances.

Motivating factors

There is a long list of what makes people feel inspired and motivated, and it could be any one of the following factors:

- recognition from peers
- praise from management
- money
- time off
- training and education
- personal development
- promotion and career progression
- travel
- future opportunities
- holidays
- continuity and staying in a comfort zone
- working hours
- nice working environment
- secure job.

What motivates you?

Name: **Date:**

This is a triangular comparison grid with the following categories listed diagonally:

- Recognition from piers [R]
- Praise from management [P]
- Money [M]
- Time Off [TO]
- Training & Education [TE]
- Personal Development [PD]
- Promotion & Career Progression [CP]
- Holidays / Travel [H]
- Future Opportunities [FO]
- Continuity & Staying in a comfort zone [C]
- Working Hours [WH]
- Nice Working Environment [NE]
- Secure Job [SJ]

Totals

Follow the lines vertically and horizontally until the box where two categories meet.

Out of the two categories, write the [code] of the one most important to you.

At the end of each line, write the total number of times that each code appears on the whole grid.

Enter the top 3 [codes] in the following boxes:

1st: 2nd: 3rd:

View online or download at www.cityandguilds.com/USM

What is critical to realise is that none of the items on the list are correct or incorrect. It is entirely personal. Just as one thing is right for one person, it may be wrong for another. People feel motivated by many things, and all that matters is that you have identified what makes a person tick. Between you, you need to have established a way of incentivising them – and forging a path of development that is agreed between you and personal to them. It is crucial that among your team, you have a great mix of all of the things on the list in order to placate and reward people individually. Just as you would not want a salon full of staff who were all motivated by holidays, it would be equally challenging to find a team of people motivated entirely by career progression.

CALCULATING LENGTH OF SERVICE

It is very useful to keep an eye on your average length of service, and staff turnover, both for use in recruitment and promotional marketing (if high), and to look to improve or address any causes if it is lower than average. At the time of writing, the average length of staff service in salons in the UK is four years, so aim far higher than that! Calculate your average to see how your salon compares.

Work out your average length of service by adding together the total number of years worked in the salon by every employee and dividing it by the total number of employees. For instance, if you have seven team members who have worked a total of 35 years between them, divide 35 by 7: the average length of staff service is five years.

CALCULATING STAFF TURNOVER

You can work out your staff turnover using the following formula:

Adding together the total number of years worked in the salon by every employee and dividing it by the total number of employees – for instance: 7 team members who have worked an average of 35 years between them = 5 years average length of staff service.

Equally, you can work out your staff turnover by simply adding up the total number of staff and then working out the number of new recruits and the number of people leaving over a year and getting an average of this movement. Simply divide that total into the total number of staff – for instance: 10 team members in total; 2 have left and 3 have joined, so an average of 2.5 have changed = 2.5/10 = 25% staff turnover.

Staff turnover $= a \div b \times 100$

a = the average of the number of people who left in the last year and the number of people who joined

b = the present total number of staff

So, if you have 10 members of staff, two people left in the last year, and three people joined:

a = the average of 2 and 3 = 2.5

b = 10

Staff turnover $= 2.5 \div 10 \times 100 = $ **25%**

Richard Ward Management Structure

Name and position	Responsibilities
Hellen Ward Joint Managing Director	Finances, HR Marketing, Branding and PR Company Development
Richard Ward Joint Managing Director	Creative Director
Julie Norman General Manager	Management of all department heads HR and finances
Gavin Hoare Salon Manager	Management of all staff and salon
Sam Good Directors P.A.	PA to RW & HW IT and vacations
Jack Reyner/Lauren Wilkins General Managers P.A.'s	PA's to JN Maintenance and online shop
Candice Barley Brand Manager	Brand Manager of Couture hair and seasons
Nando Lopes Education Director	Training and education
Mario Charalambous Technical Director	Technical and NPD (New product development)
Christiano Basciu Artistic Director	Artistic Team/Zone 1 and QVC shows
Gina Charalambous Beauty Director	Metrospa
Louise Smythe Reception Manager	Reception
Matt Hawes Zone Director	Zone 2

SALON ROLES AND RESPONSIBILITIES (TIERS)

Once you have identified those who are looking to develop and progress within the salon and want to take on more responsibility, you can involve them in the salon management system and invite them to take a more active part in the decision-making process. For instance, you could ask them to supervise junior team members and get involved in training and education, leading them to feeding back on appraisals and beginning to take more day-to-day responsibilities.

DIFFERENT DEPARTMENTAL ROLES

For each department, there are many roles that you ca≠n create to help develop your team. These include the following:

- **apprentices**: Head Junior (organises lunch breaks, etc and feeds back issues on behalf of the junior team)
- **stylists**: Head of Cutting and Styling (Head of department)
- **artistic team**: Creating an artistic team who can be responsible for photographic work, seminars, in-salon training and education can be invaluable experience for those interested in evolving their creative skills – it is also useful for encouraging a cross section of the team to pool ideas and inspire each other, so it should be open to staff across many levels (junior team members may wish to assist and watch and may aspire to be members once their training is complete)
- **technicians**: Technical Director (head of department)
- **beauty salon/spa**: Head Therapist, Head Nail Technician or Spa Director (head of department)
- **reception**: Head Receptionist.

DEPARTMENT HEADS

Each head of department can be responsible for giving feedback on any issues that involve their team: uniform, pricing structure, new treatments and services, PR, marketing, client experience issues, etc. They should be invited to attend other department head meetings regularly with you as the salon manager/owner. However, this would not apply to the position of Head Junior, who may have a separate meeting and should not be privy to the sharing of more important information which is for senior team members only.

EARNING RESPECT

Respect is not earned by having a title or wearing a badge – it is only earned through consistently practising what you preach. If anyone were to ask me why they were not afforded more respect I would insist the answer lay within themselves. You will not be awarded respect by your team for shouting the odds or developing a fiery temper; you will only be looked up to if you are firm, fair, diligent and consistent in your approach to salon management. When training up new supervisors and managers, it is vital to ensure their own personal chair-side manner with their teams conforms to your idea of good, strong salon management. Getting frustrated and impatient with people will have a negative effect. Help those interested in getting into more managerial-type positions to develop an empathetic manner and mentor them by leading by example and showing them how to embrace the 'praise – criticise – praise' ethos.

CREATING REPORTING LINES

Your team members need structure, and that includes knowing who to report to. It also helps you in delegating elements of your role if you create a chain of communication. This frees you up to deal with bigger issues by making sure your deputies or department heads are firmly in control of the day-to-day issues.

I find that it works well to tier or create levels of reporting and to stick to a rigid structure that is employed across all departments. The larger your salon, the more structure you may need. Take this example of a large salon and filter out the roles that are not applicable to your salon's size. In larger salons, it may be necessary to have a floor manager supervising the client UXP and the flow of business from operator to operator, rather like the maitre d'hotel in a top restaurant. Remember, this is just a first point of call; all serious issues should come straight to you via the supervisor or otherwise.

Areas of responsibility

Some areas of responsibility you could develop include the following:
- juniors/apprentices report to the Floor Manager (the Maitre d'hotel) or relevant department supervisor, depending on which department they are assigned to
- beauty therapists report first to the Senior or Head Therapist, or Spa Director
- stylists report to the Head of Cutting and Styling Manager or Artistic Director
- artistic team members report to the Creative Director
- technicians report to the Technical Director
- receptionists report to the Head Receptionist

- other staff (laundry, etc) report to the Salon Manager
- all department heads report to the General Manager
- General Manager and admin/secretarial staff report to the salon owner or directors.

DELEGATING RESPONSIBILITIES

The reporting lines only really work if those underneath you, who are a first point of call for any team issues, are empowered to make decisions and deal with them. This is important to filter through to the teams that they are supervising: team members will only need to speak to you if the manager or 'in between' point of contact is not in a position to act.

It is really important to back your 'number two' or head of department in front of other team members and not undermine either their responsibility or area of control. If someone comes to you about a minor issue, it is worth asking them why they felt they could not go and speak to their immediate superior about it, or why they felt it needed your input. It may be the issue has been put on the 'back burner' and their superior has not responded quickly enough, or that they were waiting for your agreement on the matter. More seriously, it may signal a lack of synergy between the supervisor and their team and training and mentoring from you may be required; whatever the reason, you need to act fast to address the feedback to the manager concerned.

Having regular meetings with your supervisory team to feed back on minor issues is vital to ensure the salon is performing well and your managerial back-up and support network feel they are being listened to and valued.

SUMMARY

The ability to discover and strengthen our team's strengths and nurture their talents is key to your job satisfaction as salon owner or manager. It is rewarding and fulfilling to see staff developing and evolving and having the ability to encourage their performance through maximising their strong points. Finding out what motivates and inspires them isequally rewarding for both you as the salon manager and them in their journey of personal discovery.

Track your staff turnover and average length of staff service – no statistics will tell you more about your salon than your ability to retain team members. Cultivate a reputation for looking after your team and recruitment interest in your brand and its reputation will increase automatically.

Creating a salon hierarchy and structure not only helps your teams understand who they can go to in your absence, but also helps to keep minor issues away from your workload and gives the staff a person who they can go to as a 'sounding board' before reaching you. It helps to motivate those who you are looking to develop and empower by giving them some responsibility; for those underneath, and coming up through the ranks, it gives them an idea of the areas where their career can develop in your company/salon.

CHAPTER 12
EFFECTIVE BOOKING SYSTEMS

This chapter will look at maximising our most precious commodity: time. We will cover the most effective booking systems you can introduce to ensure your salon is as productive, well utilised and time-managed as possible. We will look at creating 'feeding' lists of where to send your precious new clients, priority booking systems, effective appointment booking practice and the software and manual systems you can use for optimum results.

MANAGING APPOINTMENT TIMES

Perhaps one of the most critical areas in which to establish good practice is how to book clients' appointments. You need to aim to increase your productivity without lowering your standards. Remember that the longer you spend, the more you should be charging – if you go for high volumes of clients, you will charge them less but spend less time on them, too.

You must manage your appointment time expertly, always remembering that lost booking time is turnover lost forever – so developing skills to minimise any 'white space' in your appointments list is vital. Monitoring and evaluating the way you book your appointments – or sell your time – is another important aspect of your role.

The longer you spend on a client, the more you should charge.

TIME – OUR COMMODITY

If an alien landed from Mars and asked me what I did for a living I would reply that I sell the time of hair and beauty experts – because essentially, that is my job as a salon owner and manager. Whereas other companies sell products, we sell services; and those services are charged and dictated by time. As an industry, we calculate our prices by first working out each individual's hourly rate and then how long a service takes. Time governs you; it is your most precious commodity. You need to value it and teach your team to do so, and then learn how to maximise this resource, much as any other industry would maximise their greatest asset.

Importance of reception

It is therefore essential to employ a good receptionist, even in a small salon. A receptionist who is well trained and experienced can maximise appointments and optimise operators' time and, in doing so, will more than earn their salary, as well as giving a professional service and allowing other team members to concentrate solely on their roles without interruption. An inexperienced person answering the phone means that we are leaving our most precious resource in incompetent hands. This makes little business sense, gives an unprofessional image of a salon and will ultimately be bad for profitability.

WHO TO BOOK?

There is a saying in times of austerity or in challenging climates, which we would be wise to remember in boom times – **'buy once, buy well'**, or **'buy cheap, buy twice'**; so it is crucial to make sure that the customer experience, at any level, is value for money.

There are always those who will want to see the most senior operator available or book in with someone at the highest level. Similarly, there will be clients who are shopping on price, but who also want to buy into your salon ethos and brand at a lower level. There will also be a group of people who buy into the middle level as a safe option – rather as you might be if faced with buying a lawnmower from a catalogue and do not know what any of the features or benefits mean. Therefore, a tiered price list should 'tick all the boxes' and appeal to everyone who wants to experience your brand.

In each tier, there will be operators who are reaching their KPIs better than others. It makes sense to have a ranking order within each tier, with the highest achievers at the top of the list, in order to determine who to send your customers to. This should be adhered to by whoever is booking the appointment and will therefore minimise the risk of the customer failing to return.

FEEDING LISTS

A feeding list is a list that ranks operators in each tier, according to their performance and ability. Top performers are 'fed' new and transient clients first. Having a salon 'pecking order' is a great way to reward good performance, as operators who are hitting their KPIs and performance benchmarks should be nearer the top.

Obviously, the client/operator 'match-making' will invariably come into the equation, as making sure the client fits and gels with their operator is vital. However, developing a ranking order for how new or transient clients will be distributed is a great way of encouraging team members to work on their performance. Operators who improve and deliver their KPIs will see an instant benefit in their client volumes and turnover, which will benefit them financially (if their pay is performance-related).

FACTORS TO CONSIDER

A feeding list should be devised by considering a number of factors. All of these should be made clear to the team, so they are aware of how they can progress to a better position on the list and receive more bookings for transient and new clients. Think about assessing it by looking at their:

- percentage request rate/client retention skills
- occupancy rates
- customer service levels
- experience amid the relevant tier
- ability to suggest new ideas
- consultation skills
- timekeeping (both their punctuality and running their column to time)
- talent/creative ability.

How you ascertain the order of what is important to your salon is personal to you, but whatever criteria the feeding list position involves, make sure the team are aware of them and know how the 'who is positioned where' list has been decided.

Following the list

Run the columns in the same order as the feeding list. The eye is naturally drawn from left to right so the columns should flow in that direction, with the most favoured operator on the far left. Much of the time the first operator may already be booked, so simply move along to the next column and position in the feeding list and book the next available operator.

For those clients who really do not mind who they see (on any tier/level) and price is not an issue, it is obvious that it is important to book in order of seniority, with the most expensive tier first, helping to replenish our most senior operators' clienteles and therefore selling our most productive time.

Anyone booking appointments needs to be carefully trained to get the right balance between adhering to the feeding list and judging the client/operator suitability. Hence, booking appointments is a highly skilled job, and not one that should be delegated to junior team members.

PROS AND CONS OF INSTIGATING A FEEDING LIST

There are different factors to consider for and against a feeding list.

Pros

The advantages of a feeding list are as follows.

- It stimulates the right approach to hitting KPIs.
- It is a tangible benefit of good performance.
- It replenishes natural client decline for most productive operators.
- It ensures that your precious new customers visit your best available operator at all times.
- It develops the right ethos of the flow of new clients, booking by starting at the top, not the bottom of the salon hierarchy.

Cons

There are also some disadvantages of a feeding list.

- It can cause problems among the team – be sure it is judged on the right criteria.
- It needs regular re-evaluation to ensure criteria are being met on an ongoing basis, but don't be tempted to swap it around too much.
- It can require careful introduction and explanation.

PRICE TIERING AND MULTIPLE SERVICES

We have already talked about having a tiered pricing structure to appeal to a cross-section of potential salon customers and its value and appeal in encouraging a diverse client mix.

It is particularly satisfying is to see a client crossing all price boundaries and buying into different levels. For example, a hair client might opt for a premier technician for her colouring service but will reduce her total treatment cost by having a graduate stylist for the blow-dry, which she considers less important. Another client may choose a senior therapist for her waxing, but a standard therapist for her manicuring. Price tiering keeps additional services affordable and, remember, the more multiple services a customer has, the more likely they are to stay loyal and for longer.

Think of price tiering as the equivalent of hotel accommodation options; customers can choose the standard twin room, the deluxe room, the junior suite or the presidential suite – all will have quite a price differentiation between them so if the client wants to trade up and pay for more, they have the option. Developing a similar ethos in our salons is the key to successful price tiering.

PRIORITY BOOKING SYSTEMS

Time is money, so we need to prioritise it. In order to really sell our time effectively, we need to work out which periods are most likely to generate transient business and then keep them as free as possible, encouraging clients to book into quieter times that are less likely to be filled by walk-in business or last-minute bookings. This will be specific to your salon, as each business will have their own time slots that they should book as a priority to optimise their turnover.

Stylist	Amanda	23rd July
8.30		
8.45		
9.00	X	Jones
9.15		
9.30		CBD
9.45		
10.00	X	Smith
10.15		
10.30		BD
10.45		
11.00		
11.15		
11.30		
11.45		
12.00	O	Wallace
12.15		
12.30		CBD
12.45		
1.00	N	Cotton
1.15		
1.30		CBD
1.45		
2.00	O	Earnest
2.15		
2.30		BD
2.45		
3.00		
3.15		
3.30		
3.45		
4.00	X	Fredricks
4.15		
4.30		BD
4.45		
5.00		
5.15		
5.30		X 3
5.45		O 2
6.00		N 1
6.15		Total: 6
6.30		
6.45		% Request: 50%
7.00		

Example

For instance, 9am is usually a very unlikely time to get transient clients or walk-in business so, where possible and when clients are flexible, the receptionist should prioritise booking this time by suggesting the 9am slot rather than the more popular 11am slot. The 11am slot is more likely to be filled because the salon will have already been open for a few hours and the chances of walk-in trade will be far higher than at 9am. So, 9am may be a priority slot to steer a customer towards. If the client prefers to come later this is, of course, fine and the customer's choice. The system is merely to ensure that receptionists are fully aware of what times are naturally less productive and need to be filled first, when possible.

There will be other priority booking times throughout the day, so grade them in order of their importance: eg first priority at 9am, second priority 5.30pm, third priority 1pm, etc, to ensure that your unpopular times are booked first and that you will have availability to cater to any possible transient business.

EFFECTIVE APPOINTMENT BOOKING

It is well worth keeping a 'salon handbook' of all of your operators. List their personal preferences, so that receptionists can have a handy reference guide that will give them the following information.

Duration of appointments

These should be on an individual basis; for instance, cut and blow-dry time is one hour.

Days, hours and times worked

Show each operator can be flexible; for example Stylist X can stay late on a Wednesday night, if requested.

New/existing clients price differentials

Sometimes, if an operator moves up a tier, they may keep their existing clients on their previous price level for an agreed length of time before changing them to the increased rate.

Time	Booking	Notes
9.00 am	Jones	
9.15 am	CBD	*Lost time =*
9.30 am	"	*1 hr 15 mins*
9.45 am	LOST	
10.00 am	Mayhew	
10.15 am	BD	
10.30 am	LOST	
11.00 am	Smith	
11.15 am	Gent Cut	
11.30 am	LOST	
11.45 am	LOST	
12.00 pm	Norman	
12.15 pm	BD	
12.30 pm	LOST	
12.45 pm		
1.00 pm		
1.15 pm		
1.30 pm		
1.45 pm		
2.00 pm	Jones	
2.15 pm	CBD	*Gained time =*
2.30 pm	"	*1 x CBD*
2.45 pm	Mayhew	
3.00 pm	BD	
3.15 pm	Smith	
3.30 pm	Gent Cut	
3.45 pm	Norman	
4.00 pm	BD	*CBD 45 Mins*
4.15 pm	Highe's	*BD 30 Mins*
4.30 pm	CBD	*Gent 30 Mins*
4.45 pm	"	
5.00 pm		

Areas of expertise

Each operator will have their own expert or signature treatment, or flair with a particular type of client or on a technical level, which will naturally evolve. Being aware of this and marketing and promoting operators' strengths to those who are making appointments is vital.

MAXIMISING TIME

Running an effective appointment system is about maximising time. Normally, salon time is booked in 15-minute slots, but often our brains tend to work on a longer level, for example in units of half an hour or even an hour. For this reason, a client may be given a 10.00am slot rather than being offered a 9.45am appointment that would be far more productive for the salon. Teaching team members to 'squash up' appointments and avoid any wasted space is therefore key to making sure your salon time is being sold as effectively as possible. However, to do so, your salon handbook information needs to be spot on, as operator's individual times will dictate the length of their appointments and, essentially, their ability to run to time.

Remember to review your handbook during individual appraisals, to ensure information (particularly duration of services and the operator's pricing) is correct.

SOFTWARE SYSTEMS

There are many types of software on the market that can help you run your salon. There are some affordable systems that offer a monthly payment plan and which do not involve a large investment upfront.

Some will merely provide a booking system for you to use, while others will let customers book directly. There are some that will provide many reports – some of which will be more useful than others. Some systems can help you run other aspects of your business; for instance, monitoring and controlling stock through using a barcode scanner. It is vital that you choose an affordable system that fits your individual salon's requirements. The most important function of your system will be recording and sorting client histories and technical data, such as colour formulas and so on. Conventional pen and paper record cards are not as secure as they need to be, and information can easily be copied or lost from them if an operator is thinking of moving and taking their clients with them.

Whatever software you choose, make sure it tracks the KPIs you are judging your team performance on: percentage request, occupancy rates, takings and so on, and also ensure that it breaks down your turnover by department. You really only need a couple of reports so choose a system that provides you with what you need to know. It should also be able to offer the services you need, such as text messaging, as well as providing you with the security you need to protect the delicate information it stores.

MANUAL SYSTEMS

The pen and paper system still has its place for plenty of salon owners across the UK. However, there are drawbacks in using the 'old fashioned' way, namely keeping and filing records for your audit trail and accounting practice. Storing of manual files is bulky and requires adequate space, and booking sheets can get lost or damaged (not good news for your HMRC inspection!).

RECORDING THE KPIs MANUALLY

It is crucial to identify your clients at the point of booking. Knowing if they are new, regular or transient, and monitoring them is essential to provide the data with which you are judging the operators' KPIs.

If you are not computerised, you can still track this by using an identifying or colour coding system and reference at the time of booking, for example:

- request is marked by circling the appointment time with an R
- transient is marked by circling the appointment time with a T
- new clients are identified by circling the appointment time with an N.

All clients can then be marked off manually using a highlighter pen system:

- pink for request
- green for transient
- yellow for new.

At the end of each day, you can simply tot up the numbers of request, transient and new customers. To calculate the request rate, divide the total number of requests into the total number to ascertain the percentage request rate.

For instance, 5 request clients, 2 transient and 1 new = 8 total clients.

5 divided by 8 = 62.5% request rate for that day.

Of course, this then needs to be calculated weekly, monthly and annually for assessment and appraisal, as does the other key information such as takings, retail sales, average bill and occupancy rate.

Pen and paper bookings make gleaning information for your KPIs harder, but not impossible.

STANDING APPOINTMENTS

In years gone by, most salons had Friday time slots which were full of clients who came at the same time every week. This was known as a standing appointment – a regular appointment booked on the same day of every week at the same time. Unfortunately, this trend is in decline and the regular weekly booking is becoming a thing of the past. We should aim to reinvigorate this trend and start to encourage the clients who have a weekly blow-dry or manicure visit into booking a regular time slot on a regular day, if at all possible, and encouraging the prebooking of a regular appointment. Knowing that our operators' time is already paid for is a comfort most salon owners or managers (and operators) would relish!

CANCELLATION POLICIES

It is now standard for any companies who are selling time to have a cancellation policy in place. It is advisable to ask for 24 hours' notice of cancellation for customers cancelling their appointments. Most dentists and other appointment-based enterprises require this now, so it is seeping into the British customer mindset more and more; as such it should be easier for salons to initiate as time goes on. Most hotels or top restaurants would charge for missed reservations, so we should aim to develop the same policy.

If you are nervous about instigating such a policy, start by donating a percentage of your cancellation fees to charity, to establish the right attitude towards the fee. Your team should be pleased to see it come to force if 'no shows' are a problem in your salon, so get them involved in the process of introducing the policy.

Making clients aware

You could adopt a policy of making sure clients are fully aware of any applicable fees through the following procedures.

- Remind them at the time of booking that failure to give 24 hours' notice of cancellation may result in a fee being charged.
- Take deposits for long bookings (more than two hours' duration) or for new clients. Tell clients that a credit card number is required to secure their booking, and the card will only be charged if they fail to adhere to the cancellation policy (you must have the right **EPOS systems** in place for this).
- Steer multiple appointments towards quieter days – hopefully avoiding the nightmare scenario of a client booked for a whole day of services on a Saturday who then fails to show. Even though some of the time may get filled, the resulting wasted time is a risk to profitability and turnover.
- Call or text clients to remind them of their bookings, particularly long appointments, which require confirmation.
- Give them a second chance if they do forget to turn up for an appointment, if appropriate. It is not worth losing a client over something out of their control, but habitual 'no show' clients do more harm than good!

EPOS system

An electronic point of sale system.

CLIENT WAITING LIST

Keep a daily list under each column of clients waiting for appointments so you can fill any cancelled bookings. It makes for great customer service and effectively enables you to sell the time twice if fees apply.

RECEPTION'S ROLE

The all-important rebooking of appointments is vital, so ensure that your reception team is well versed in offering the client the chance to follow up their treatment plan and rebook before they leave. Also, remind the receptionist of the part they play in up-selling, link-selling and cross-referring. They can be very effective in suggesting ancillary treatments and services, especially where there are potential time delays or mistakes that result in clients having to wait. Offering additional (discounted) services to appease any ill-feeling due to salon-induced errors can be a great way of introducing clients to services and treatments which are new to them.

SUMMARY

Teaching all the team about the importance of selling time is vital to utilising your most vital commodity. It is key to get operators to think in the right way; make everybody aware that lost time is irreplaceable money and means resulting lost income.

Developing and establishing the right systems to ensure each column is as well-utilised and productive as possible will ensure that the salon is operating to its optimum capacity. Regular re-evaluation of your procedures is essential to keep the team motivated and well informed.

In encouraging your teams to adopt a 'time-is-money' ethos towards their column and its productivity, it is also worth encouraging a cancellation policy and training, and educating your clients that turning up for an appointment is merely expected salon protocol.

STEPS FOR SUCCESS

10 STEPS FOR MAXIMISING TEAM PERFORMANCE

1　Time is our industry commodity, aim to increase efficiency without compromising standards.

2　Offer value for money – don't over-promise or under-deliver.

3　Staff investment, training and performance building will pay off financially. Grow your team and deliver an ethos they believe in.

4　Cultivate the ongoing learning experience; educate, motivate, communicate, delegate. Train and teach 'your way' continually.

5　Know yourself, know your business, know your team, know your client.

6　Nurture and take care of those who work for you and you'll succeed on their achievements.

7　Team autonomy and empowerment = real business success. Build your team, then trust them to get on with it. Don't micromanage.

8　Address issues and confront problems; don't let them fester. If staff-related, praise – criticise – praise.

9　Brand values evolve naturally – they are an ethos not a design decision.

10　Focus on your UXP (user experience). Keep making sure it is better and better.

EPILOGUE

You made it!

You should now know everything you need to manage or own a hair and beauty salon – and to get the results you need. I have shared with you the knowledge that it has taken me more than 25 years to glean in order to deliver guaranteed results and give you some understanding of every area you need to get to grips with to run your business profitably, professionally and productively.

Hair and beauty salons are like any other companies: you need to make money and be profitable and you do not have to sidestep this issue or apologise for it. Sometimes, team members get a warped understanding of our highly personal service industry and get their wires a little crossed – thinking that they are performing a public service, when they are actually employed to help us make money. We are not carers, care home assistants, or hospital workers; we are categorised as being in the retail sector and we need to be ever more commercially minded if we are going to find our salon's niche in such a competitive sector. Embracing and acting on the customer feedback you (hopefully) now continue to ask for, will be invaluable.

I hope that this series of books will encourage you to create your own management systems (I would love to hear about them) or establish your own good working practice that will deliver results. Remember, you are a business person (even if you are running a column) and you have a certain skill set in order to do the job you are doing, which you have the power to keep on developing, in order to be the best you can be. Keep remembering our '-ate' words: communicate, educate, motivate, delegate. You can never do enough of all four if you want to get the best results.

It is not easy being the boss – it can be a lonely place. Leading a team needs dedication and commitment and, sometimes, there are challenges that you can only face alone, so maintaining your self belief is critical – stay motivated! Trust your instinct and go with your gut feeling; but remember never to be impulsive, think carefully and consider options before jumping in too quickly, and sleep on your big decisions. However, addressing concerns immediately is a vital management tool. Confront those difficult issues and they will not seem so bad. Your persistence and perseverance will be the key to your success.

Our climate is ever-changing, so some areas will require further research when you refer to these books as a reference guide, as invariably there will be updated information and changes to tax rates, legislation, etc. Part of your job as a salon manager or owner is to keep yourself updated. The onus is increasingly on the proprietor or manager to be well-informed, hence the complexity and detail in this guide. Even if some of what is written in the series does not end up affecting you, it is good to know about – knowledge can only ever be power. Good luck!

Contact me at: hellen@ultimatesalonmanagement.com

INDEX